LIBRARY -
1978
2 1765 0000
D1551542

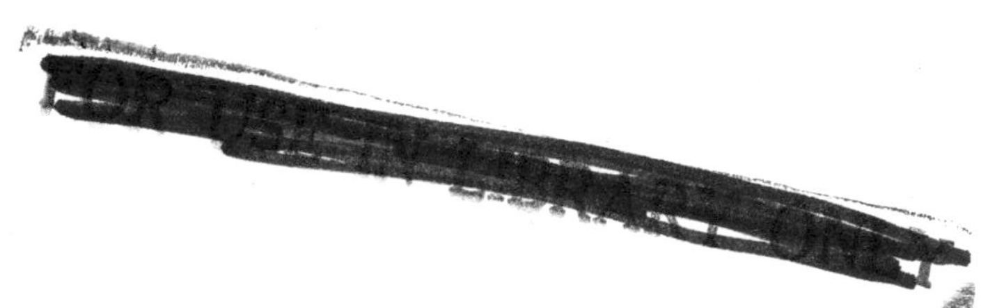

The Scarecrow Author Bibliographies

1. John Steinbeck (Tetsumaro Hayashi). 1973.
2. Joseph Conrad (Theodore G. Ehrsam). 1969.
3. Arthur Miller (Tetsumaro Hayashi). 2d ed. 1976.
4. Katherine Anne Porter (Waldrip & Bauer). 1969.
5. Philip Freneau (Philip M. Marsh). 1970.
6. Robert Greene (Tetsumaro Hayashi). 1971.
7. Benjamin Disraeli (R. W. Stewart). 1972.
8. John Berryman (Richard W. Kelly). 1972.
9. William Dean Howells (Vito J. Brenni). 1973.
10. Jean Anouilh (Kathleen W. Kelly). 1973.
11. E. M. Forster (Alfred Borrello). 1973.
12. The Marquis de Sade (E. Pierre Chanover). 1973.
13. Alain Robbe-Grillet (Dale W. Frazier). 1973.
14. Northrop Frye (Robert D. Denham). 1974.
15. Federico García Lorca (Laurenti & Siracusa). 1974.
16. Ben Jonson (Brock & Welsh). 1974.
17. Four French Dramatists: Eugène Brieux, François de Curel, Emile Fabre, Paul Hervieu (Edmund F. Santa Vicca). 1974.
18. Ralph Waldo Ellison (Jacqueline Covo). 1974.
19. Philip Roth (Bernard F. Rodgers, Jr.). 1974.
20. Norman Mailer (Laura Adams). 1974.
21. Sir John Betjeman (Margaret Stapleton). 1974.
22. Elie Wiesel (Molly Abramowitz). 1974.
23. Paul Laurence Dunbar (Eugene W. Metcalf, Jr.). 1975.
24. Henry James (Beatrice Ricks). 1975.
25. Robert Frost (Lentricchia & Lentricchia). 1976.
26. Sherwood Anderson (Douglas G. Rogers). 1976.
27. Iris Murdoch and Muriel Spark (Tominaga & Schneidermeyer). 1976.
28. John Ruskin (Kirk H. Beetz). 1976.
29. Georges Simenon (Trudee Young). 1976.
30. George Gordon, Lord Byron (Oscar José Santucho). 1976.
31. John Barth (Richard Vine). 1977.
32. John Hawkes (Carol A. Hryciw). 1977.
33. William Everson (Bartlett & Campo). 1977.
34. May Sarton (Lenora Blouin). 1978.
35. Wilkie Collins (Kirk H. Beetz). 1978.
36. Sylvia Plath (Lane & Stevens). 1978.
37. E. B. White (A. J. Anderson). 1978.
38. Henry Miller (Lawrence J. Shifreen). 1978.

MAY SARTON:

A Bibliography

by

Lenora P. Blouin

The Scarecrow Author Bibliographies, No. 34

The Scarecrow Press, Inc.
Metuchen, N.J. & London
1978

Library of Congress Cataloging in Publication Data

Blouin, Lenora P
May Sarton : a bibliography.

(The Scarecrow author bibliographies ; no. 34)
Bibliography: p.
Includes index.
1. Sarton, May, 1912- --Bibliography.
Z8784.43.B58 [PS3537.A832] 016.811'5'2 77-14311
ISBN 0-8108-1054-9

Manufactured in the United States of America

To the one who had faith in me

TABLE OF CONTENTS

PREFACE

Initially, when formulating the idea of a bibliography on May Sarton, I envisioned a simple, two-part division of works by her and works about her, but as I began to gather material I realized that the quantity alone would necessitate a more complicated format. Overall, there are still two main divisions, but within each there are several subdivisions to accommodate the various types of writing.

The first major division, works by Sarton, is arranged into subdivisions by genre: poetry; novels; non-fiction; etc., the exception being two subdivisions (individual poems not in published volumes and translations of individual poems) which are arranged in chronological order by date of publication.

The second major division, works about Sarton, has been divided into specific book reviews and general, biographical/critical articles. The book reviews are organized by genre, followed by the title of the work being reviewed and the name of the critic, in alphabetical order. Although I have included some major British reviews, the emphasis is on American criticism, mainly due to its availability in most public or academic libraries in the United States. The biographical/critical entries, more than book reviews, include material about Sarton's life in relation to her work, as well as examining several works in relation to a theme or themes in her writing.

Following the body of the bibliography I have included, as an appendix, a partial checklist of Sarton's individual poems, listed in alphabetical order by title, followed by their location(s). I have tried to make the checklist as complete as possible but because of the quantity of her writing, much of it in obscure or out-of-print journals, and because of the arbitrariness of indexes, some titles may have been missed.

With the annotations I attempted to follow the advice

of the American Library Association's Bibliography Committee:

> Abstracts should give enough of the contents to enable the user to decide accurately whether he wants to read the original.... In each case they should be succinct....

For the most part I hoped to include those sentences or paragraphs which would indicate whether the review was negative or positive, yet, at the same time, keep the annotation as brief as possible. It was not my intent to alter or change the tone or meaning of the book review or critical article but only to provide a summary of its contents.

I cannot claim an error-free bibliography, but, as much as possible, I have tried to be complete and accurate. It could not have been as complete without the continual support and assistance of May Sarton. From the beginning she has provided articles, poems, reviews and other material, as well as suggestions and encouragement. Libraries, both public and academic, have extended their services by way of providing material and information. I wish to especially thank Santa Clara Public Library, San Francisco Public Library, Scripps College Library, Harvard University Library, New York Public Library and the Library of Congress for their assistance.

Finally, I wish to thank friends for their continual support and encouragement, especially Sharon, who helped revise and edit some of the material.

L. P. B.

INTRODUCTION

The 1976 release of May Sarton's work, A World of Light: Portraits and Celebrations, marked her forty-sixth year of writing for publication. Her novels, poetry, essays, memoirs, and short stories number in the hundreds and span several generations, yet her works have never been collected or organized into an extensive bibliography, or any detailed list which would facilitate the study and research of her literary development. Quantity alone does not necessitate a bibliography, but quality does, and very few readers would deny that there is quality in Sarton's writing. The enduring power of her works attests to this quality, as does her ability to capture the essence of her experiences and relate them through fiction, poetry and memoirs.

The growing interest in Sarton's work is due, in part, to the current search by women for their own viable identity. What renders this interest surprising is the fact that this search, for Sarton, is not a new one; her earliest writings were concerned with the importance of woman's self-exploration and actualization. In such novels as The Bridge of Years (1946), Shower of Summer Days (1952) and The Birth of a Grandfather (1957) her leading women characters grow to understand themselves in relation to their husbands, friends or lovers. Other works were equally concerned with the role of the artist, specifically the female artist, in society. Even though, in many cases, the protagonist in her novels (whether poet, teacher, painter or writer) is a woman, the emphasis is not placed on the sex of the individual, but rather on the vision and understanding of self. Sarton believes that the importance for the individual lies in choosing a life for himself/herself rather than blindly accepting assigned sex roles. For example, Mark, in The Single Hound (1938), was able to meet and relate to the fact that the writer he had admired as Jean Latour was in reality a woman.

In her introduction to the 1974 edition of Sarton's novel Mrs. Stevens Hears the Mermaids Singing, Carolyn

Heilbrun touches on Sarton's attitudes towards homosexuality, both in this novel and in her personal life. Heilbrun believes, and rightly so, that the homosexuality is not the most important point of consideration:

> Sarton knows ... how many women writers have had homosexual lovers, and I think the matter is not of particular importance here, except to suggest that it is about time we got such matters in better perspective.[1]

For Heilbrun the consideration of it is important only because, "... the subject with all its history and hysteria and social overtones comes between the writer and his work and between him and the reader."[2] I would suggest it is also important because, even though most artists have their personal muses which serve as a catalyst for their creativity, for the homosexual, especially the female, Sarton's understanding of homosexuality and her sympathetic treatment of it are strong points of reference; she intelligently and artistically presents an "unsensational" point of view. Heilbrun writes:

> ... Mrs. Stevens ... is outstanding because its homosexuality is not seen in its social or shocking aspects at all. It is used thematically to discover the source of poetry for the woman artist.[3]

Solitude is a prevalent theme in May Sarton's works. Living in solitude, for her, is a conscious choice and a state in which she learns to look within herself, seeing both her strengths and weaknesses. The need to be alone became a driving force in her life, partly because it allowed her the freedom to work without interruption, and partly because it gave her time to think and work without feeling obligated to recognize the presence and demands of another person.

> Loneliness is most acutely felt with other people, for with others even with a lover sometimes, we suffer from our differences, differences of taste, temperament, mood. Human intercourse often demands that we soften the edge of perception or withdraw at the very instant of personal truth for fear of hurting, or being inappropriately present ... in a social situation.[4]

From Journal of a Solitude (1973), Sarton's sustained statement of "aloneness," we learn that this solitude has not always facilitated a feeling of peace. An inner turmoil, best expressed in her poem "Gestalt at Sixty," may also be present:

> I can tell you that solitude
> Is not all exaltation, inner space
> Where the soul breathes and work can be done.
> Solitude exposes the nerve,
> Raises up ghosts,
> The past, never at rest, flows through it.[5]

With the publication of Plant Dreaming Deep (1968) May Sarton gained wide recognition among her readers as a sensitive, gentle woman who quietly lived a life as a writer and gardener, removed from the world of strife and chaos. This image was incomplete and, in a sense, misleading. What of her anger, fear, passion, anguish and self-doubt? These were a part of her daily life as much as the gentleness and sensitivity. It was partly because of this misconception that Sarton wrote Journal of a Solitude, to dispel the myth of total serenity. Her journal expressed this passion and anger, and in spite of disappointing some romantics, revealed a more complete, complex woman. This passionate and volatile side of her personality was not something new just to her later years; it had always been there, even in earlier works. One of her first published sonnets contained these lines:

> Love never was fulfillment of desire.
> Love is not anything that has been said.
> I curse it, knowing well that the same thirst
> Will turn me back to bless what I have cursed.[6]

Although May Sarton is a prolific and experienced writer of both the novel and the poem, the latter has remained her primary passion and concern. It is not that she believes the poem to be "better" than the novel (they both have important literary functions to perform, she contends) but the feelings experienced after completing a poem can be more fulfilling for her than after completing a novel:

> The novel can and usually does deal with growth and change; time is of its essence. Whereas the poem is timeless. So the novel requires a long breath, the sustained ever-renewed effort. Per-

> haps that is why ... I never feel the elation that I experience when a poem is finished. I am simply relieved to lay down the burden and be done with it.[7]

Encounter in April, her first volume of poetry, was published in 1937. Since that year she has written and published ten volumes of verse, as well as many individual poems in magazines, newspapers, and anthologies. Her poetry covers the range from traditional verse forms to free verse, but within the past several years she has become recognized for her powerfully mature sonnet sequences. Referring to the traditional forms of verse Sarton insists that one must be thoroughly familiar with them before a rejection or substitution may be made for free forms. In an essay entitled "A Poet's Letter to a Beginner" she writes:

> Craft is the means by which we create the illusion of 'the naked raw stuff.' If you choose to deny yourself all the magic and charms that severe forms release for a reader, you have got to find a substitute for them.[8]

The current substitute of "shock language" and violence in contemporary poetry, it is hoped, cannot be a lasting one, Sarton writes, because "... one of the great values of poetry is that it provides an indefinitely renewable experience."[9] Like Matthew Arnold's argument for high standards of literary judgment, using the "lines and expressions of the great masters ... as a touchstone to other poetry,"[10] May Sarton believes it is important for the poet to be familiar with the previous generations of great poets. One does not write from a vacuum, but, rather, draws upon the ideas of former writers and incorporates their ideas into one's own writing. This does not mean one imitates earlier poets, (Sarton notes, "influence is not imitation") but it means a writer should reach back in time to poets such as Donne, Milton, Hopkins and others and absorb their words. In this way the young poet can discover his or her own voice by allowing a fertilization from a poet established in literary history.

As is true of younger poets, Sarton's early writing was influenced by other, more established poets. The sonnet sequence "Encounter in April" from her first volume of poetry by the same name contains sonnets which reveal a strong influence from Edna St. Vincent Millay. Gradually this obvious influence fades from Sarton's poetry as she begins to develop her own poetic voice. The sequence "Divorce of Lovers" (Cloud, Stone, Sun, Vine) and the more recent "Autumn Sonnets" (A Durable Fire) attest to her originality and mature technical ability.

Writing poetry is a serious discipline for May Sarton. She does not approach it as a time-filler or an intellectual game; poetry is necessary to her survival. "For the writing of poetry is first of all a way of life, and only secondarily a means of expression."[11] Now, after forty plus years of writing, she clearly knows her choice:

> I ponder it again and know for sure/
> My life has asked not love but poetry/[12]

Examined as a whole, the body of May Sarton's writing is almost overwhelming. It reveals an artist who has not remained stagnant or afraid of change. "Truth," especially the truth within herself, has been her life-long quest. The search for it has not been without pain or suffering, nor even without self-doubt, but her loyalty to truth has given her glimpses of a serenity seldom experienced.

> I am moving
> Toward a new freedom
> Both of detachment,
> And a sweeter grace---
> Learning to let go.
>
> I am not ready to die.
> But as I approach sixty
> I turn my face toward the sea.
> I shall go where tides replace time,
> Where my world will open to a far horizon
> Over the floating, never-still flux and change.
> I shall go with the changes,
> I shall look far out over golden grasses
> And blue waters....
>
> There are no farewells.[13]

NOTES

1. Carolyn Heilbrun. Introduction to Mrs. Stevens Hears the Mermaids Singing. (New York: W. W. Norton & Co., 1974), xvii.

2. Ibid.

3. Ibid.

4. May Sarton. "The Rewards of Living a Solitary Life," New York Times, April 8, 1974, p. 35.

5. May Sarton. "Gestalt at Sixty," in A Durable Fire. (New York: W. W. Norton & Co., 1972), 11.

6. May Sarton. "Sonnet #6," in Encounter in April. (Boston: Houghton Mifflin Co., 1937), 72.

7. May Sarton. "The Practice of Two Crafts," Christian Science Monitor, June 25, 1974, p. F7.

8. May Sarton. "A Poet's Letter to a Beginner," Writer. 75 (April, 1962), 20.

9. Ibid. (Emphasis hers.)

10. The Reader's Encyclopedia. 2nd ed., ed. William Rose Benet. (New York: Thomas Y. Crowell Co., 1965), p. 52.

11. May Sarton. The Writing of a Poem. (Scripps College, 1957), 2.

12. May Sarton. "Sonnet, #8" from the sequence "The Autumn Sonnets," in A Durable Fire, (New York: W. W. Norton & Co., 1972), 45.

13. May Sarton. "Gestalt at Sixty," op. cit., pp. 13-14.

PART I:

WORKS BY MAY SARTON

It is my hope that all the novels, the books of poems, and the autobiographical works may come to be seen as a whole, the communication of a vision of life that is unsentimental, humorous, passionate, and, in the end, timeless. We can bear any Hell if we can 'break through' to each other and come to understand ourselves.

May Sarton

VOLUMES OF POETRY

ENCOUNTER IN APRIL
Boston: Houghton Mifflin, Co., 1937.

Contents:

First Snow, p. 1.

Encounter in April, p. 5 (includes five sonnets:)
We came together softly like two deer/ p. 7.
'No spring can be eternal, nor can this'/ p. 7.
If I have poured myself without reserve/ p. 8.
For you a leopard-word--no deer, no pheasant/ p. 8.
Not without grace and certainly with pride/ p. 9.

'She Shall Be Called Woman,' p. 11.

Landscapes and Portraits, p. 23.
On the Atlantic, p. 23.
From Cornwall, p. 26.
The Trees, p. 27.
Week End, p. 28.
Kew, p. 29.
On Hampshire Downs, p. 30.
Nursery Rhyme, p. 31.
Evening Landscape, p. 33.
For Mariette Lydis, p. 34.
Portrait by Holbein, p. 35.
Portrait of One Person, p. 36.
Portrait of the Artist, p. 37.
Portraits of Three Women, p. 38.
For Eleonora Duse, p. 40.
Mountain Interval, p. 42.

Fall of Petals, p. 47.
Request, p. 49.
Japanese Papers, p. 50.
Hands, p. 53.

INNER LANDSCAPE
Boston: Houghton, Mifflin Co., 1939.
London: Cresset Press, Ltd., 1939.

Contents: (Houghton, Mifflin edition)

Sonnets:

Is this heart, emperor, setting at your feet/ p. 14.
Not for my sake who have desired it so/ p. 15.
I had not dreamed this touch would turn to stone/ p. 16.
But touch is means and signifies no more/ p. 17.
Oh child look down, look down, your open eyes/ p. 18.
For you who should have stood beside me here/ p. 19.
Alone I may be, but still twice aware/ p. 20.
Because this strange adventure is so grave/ p. 21.
Deny the passion that is bound in you/ p. 22.
There is no strength of words, none hard and pure/ p. 23.
Defeat, here where we need not move nor speak/ p. 24.
Yet pluck out from this nettle a brave flower/ p. 25.

Summary

Summary, p. 28.
Conversation on the Telephone, p. 29.
Address to the Heart, p. 31.
Transition, p. 32.
Translation, p. 33.
The Vanquished, p. 34.
Memory of Swans, p. 35.
After Silence, p. 36.

Canticles:

Behind what little mirror lies the country of your voice?/ p. 38.
As music in a still house out of silence springs/ p. 39.
Passion like radium is luminous in essence/ p. 40.
The wind which swept the earth has mounted the trees/ p. 41.
If there is mercy it is not, no, not in the wind/ p. 42.
Alone one is never lonely: the spirit adventures, waking,/ p. 43.
To stand on the earth again is a grave event/ p. 44.
That night we went outside the gate beyond the wood/ p. 45.
There are voices in the garden. Day folds itself into/ p. 46.
The spirit comes back to silence like a dove/ p. 47.

We sat smoking at a table by the river/ p. 48.
Now it is evening coming and you are not here/ p. 49.
It is a flower pressed or a perfect leaf/ p. 50.

Winter Landscape
From Men Who Died Deluded, p. 52.
Afternoon on Washington Street, p. 53.
The Puritan, p. 54.
From a Train Window, p. 55.
Static Landscape, p. 56.
Considerations, p. 57.
Winter Evening, p. 58.
Map for Despair, p. 59.
You Who Ask Peace, p. 60.
The Pride of Trees, p. 61.
Greeting, p. 62.

A Letter to James Stephens, p. 63.

THE LION AND THE ROSE
New York: Rinehart & Co., 1948.
Toronto: Clarke, Irwin & Co., 1948.

Contents: (Rinehart & Co., edition)

Theme and Variations
Meditation in Sunlight, p. 3.
Difficult Scene, p. 5.
The Window, p. 7.
The Lion and the Rose, p. 8.

American Landscapes
Winchester, Virginia, p. 13.
Monticello, p. 15.
In Deep Concern, p. 16.
Charleston Plantations, p. 17.
Where the Peacock Cried, p. 18.
In Texas, p. 20.
Boulder Dam, p. 22.
Colorado Mountains, p. 23.
Of the Seasons, p. 24.
Indian Dances, p. 26.
Santos: New Mexico, p. 28.
Poet in Residence (includes five poems:)
The Students, p. 30.
Campus, p. 31.
Before Teaching, p. 32.

THE LEAVES OF THE TREE
Mount Vernon, Iowa: Cornell College Chapbooks, 1950.

<u>Contents</u>:

LAND OF SILENCE AND OTHER POEMS
New York: Rinehart & Co., 1953.
Toronto: Clarke, Irwin & Co., 1953.

Contents: (Rinehart & Co., edition)

V

VI

IN TIME LIKE AIR

New York: Rinehart & Co., 1958.
Toronto: Clarke, Irwin & Co., 1958.

Contents: (Rhinehart & Co., edition)

A Celebration, p. 9.

I

Islands and Wells, p. 15.
Dialogue, p. 16.
The Furies, p. 18.
The Action of the Beautiful, p. 20.
On Being Given Time, p. 21.
The Metaphysical Garden, p. 22.
Lady with a Falcon, p. 26.
Where Dream Begins, p. 27.
Lament for Toby, p. 28.

II

Green Song, p. 31.
The Return, p. 32.
The Fall, p. 33.
The Olive Grove, p. 35.
Mediterranean, p. 36.
At Muzot, p. 37.
To the North, p. 38.
After Four Years, p. 39.
Somersault, p. 41.
The Frog, That Naked Creature, p. 42.
The Phoenix, p. 44.

III

In Time Like Air, p. 49.
Nativity, p. 51.
Annunciation, p. 52.
Sun Boat, p. 53.
Ceremony, p. 54.
All Souls, p. 56.
Lifting Stones, p. 57.

IV

Binding the Dragon, p. 61.
Song: Come Let us dance, my love/ p. 62.
The Fall, p. 63.

The Other Place, p. 64.
Definition, p. 65.
Fore Thought, p. 65.
A Pair of Hands, p. 66.
My Father's Death, p. 66.
The Light Years, p. 67.
Spring Day, p. 68.
By Moonlight, p. 69.
Reflections in a Double Mirror, p. 71.
Death and the Lovers, p. 72.

Translations from the French:
Allusion to Poets (Odilon-Jean Perier), p. 75.
Gifts (Francis Jammes), p. 76.
This Peasant's Son (Francis Jammes), p. 77.
Sonnet (Jean Cassou), p. 78.
Life That Passes (Pierre Seghers), p. 79.
The Voyages (Robert Sabatier), p. 80.

CLOUD, STONE, SUN, VINE: POEMS SELECTED AND NEW
New York: W. W. Norton & Co., 1961.
Toronto: George J. McLeod, Ltd., 1961.

<u>Contents</u>: (W. W. Norton & Co., edition)

Prayer before Work, p. 15.

American Places:
A New Mexican Sequence, p. 19.
Meditation in Sunlight, p. 19.
Without the Violence, p. 21.
The Land of Silence, p. 22.
Letter to an Indian Friend, p. 23.
Colorado Mountains, p. 25.
Winchester, Virginia, p. 26.
Charleston Plantations, p. 27.
Monticello, p. 28.

"O Saisons! O Chateaux!,"
Homage to Flanders, p. 31.
Summer Music, p. 33.
After a Train Journey, p. 34.
Evening in France, p. 35.
Provence, p. 36.
The Olive Grove, p. 38.
Italian Garden, p. 39.

Roman Head, p. 40.
To the North, p. 41.
"O Saisons! O Chateaux!," p. 42.
For All the Journeys, p. 43.

The Action of the Beautiful
Annunciation, p. 47.
Granted This World, p. 48.
The Action of the Beautiful, p. 49.
Evening Music, p. 50.
The Lady and the Unicorn, p. 51.
Song: This is the love I bring/ p. 52.
The Metaphysical Garden, p. 53.

The Sacred Wood
On Being Given Time, p. 59.
Sun Boat, p. 60.
At the Bottom of the Green Field, p. 61.
The Work of Happiness, p. 62.
At Muzot, p. 63.
Boy by the Waterfall, p. 64.
The Sacred Wood, p. 65.
Lifting Stone, p. 66.

Leaves before the Wind
The Swans, p. 69.
Prothalamion, p. 70.
Leaves before the Wind, p. 71.
In a Dry Land, p. 72.
The Fall, p. 73.
Now Voyager, p. 74.
A Pair of Hands, p. 75.
Spring Day, p. 76.
The Light Years, p. 77.
Death and the Lovers, p. 78.
These Images Remain (includes the following sonnets:)
These images remain, these classic landscapes/ p. 79.
The stone withstands: the chisel does destroy/ p. 79.
What angel can I leave, gentle and stern/ p. 80.
Here are the peaceful days we never knew/ p. 80.
But parting is return, the coming home/ p. 81.
In Time Like Air, p. 82.

Binding the Dragon
Humpty Dumpty, p. 85.

A PRIVATE MYTHOLOGY

New York: W. W. Norton & Co., 1966.
Toronto: George J. McLeod, 1966.
New York: W. W. Norton & Co., 1967 (paperback)

Contents: (W. W. Norton & Co., 1966 edition)

A Nobleman's House, p. 27.
Inn at Kyoto, p. 28.
An Exchange of Gifts, p. 30.
The Stone Garden, p. 32.
Wood, Paper, Stone, p. 34.
The Approach--Calcutta, p. 37.
Notes from India, p. 38.
The Great Plain of India Seen from the Air, p. 43.
In Kashmir, p. 45.
The Sleeping God, p. 46.
Birthday on the Acropolis, p. 47.
Nostalgia for India, p. 50.
A Greek Meal, p. 51.
On Patmos, p. 53.
Another Island, p. 54.
At Lindos, p. 55.
At Delphi, p. 57.
Pastoral, p. 59.
Ballads of the Traveler, p. 60.
Lazarus, p. 63.

A Private Mythology II
Heureux qui, comme Ulysse ..., p. 65.
Of Havens, p. 66.
The House in Winter, p. 67.
Still Life in Snowstorm, p. 68.
A Fugue of Wings, p. 69.
An Observation, p. 71.
Learning about Water, p. 72.
An Artesian Well, p. 74.
A Late Mowing, p. 76.
A Country Incident, p. 77.
Second Thoughts on the Abstract Gardens of Japan, p. 78.

The Animal World
A Village Tale, p. 83.
The Horse-Pulling, p. 85.
Franz, a Goose, p. 87.
Lovers at the Zoo, p. 88.
The Great Cats and the Bears, p. 90.
Turtle, p. 90.
Death and the Turtle, p. 91.

Elegies and Celebrations
Elegy, p. 95.
Death of a Psychiatrist, p. 97.

AS DOES NEW HAMPSHIRE
New Hampshire: Richard R. Smith, 1967.

Contents:

A GRAIN OF MUSTARD SEED
New York: W. W. Norton & Co., 1971.
Toronto: George J. McLeod, Ltd., 1971.

New York: W. W. Norton & Co., 1971 (paperback)

Contents: (W. W. Norton & Co., edition)

Part One
Ballad of the Sixties, p. 11.
The Rock in the Snowball, p. 13.
The Ballad of Ruby, p. 14.
The Ballad of Johnny, 16.
Easter, 1968, p. 18.
The Invocation to Kali:
The Kingdom of Kali, pp. 19-20.
The Concentration Camps, pp. 20-21.
The Time of Burning, pp. 22-23.
After the Tiger, p. 24.
"We'll to the woods no more," p. 26.
Night Watch, p. 27.

Part Two
Proteus, p. 33.
A Last Word, p. 34.
Girl with 'Cello, p. 36.
An Intruder, p. 37.
The Muse as Medusa, p. 38.
A Seventy-fifth Birthday, p. 39.
The Great Transparencies, p. 40.
Friendship: The Storms, p. 41.
Evening Walk in France, p. 42.
Dutch Interior, p. 43.
A Vision of Holland, p. 44.

Part Three
Bears and Waterfalls, p. 47.
A Parrot, p. 49.
Frogs and Photographers, p. 50.
Eine Kleine Snailmusik, p. 51.
The Fig, p. 52.
Hawaiian Palm, p. 53.

Part Four
A Hard Death, p. 57.
The Silence, p. 59.
Annunciation, p. 61.
At Chartres, p. 62.
Once More at Chartres, p. 63.
Jonah, p. 64.
Easter Morning, p. 65.

A DURABLE FIRE

New York: W. W. Norton & Co., 1972.
New York: W. W. Norton & Co., 1972 (paperback).
Toronto: George J. McLeod, Ltd., 1972.

Contents: (W. W. Norton & Co., edition)

This was our testing year after the first/ p. 46.
We watched the waterfalls, rich and baroque/ p. 46.
For steadfast flame wood must be seasoned/ p. 47.

Part Three
February Days, p. 51.
Note to a Photographer, p. 52.
March in New England, p. 53.
The Garden of Childhood, p. 54.
Composition, p. 55.
Autumn Again, p. 56.
Winter Carol, p. 57.

Part Four
Burial, p. 61.
Of Grief, p. 62.
Prisoner at a Desk, p. 64.
Birthday Present, p. 65.
Elegy for Louise Bogan, p. 66.

Part Five: Letters to a Psychiatrist
Christmas Letter, 1970, p. 69.
The Fear of Angels, p. 72.
The Action of Therapy, p. 73.
I Speak of Change, p. 78.
Easter, 1971, p. 79.
The Contemplation of Wisdom, p. 80.

COLLECTED POEMS: 1930-1973
New York: W. W. Norton & Co., 1974.
Toronto: George J. McLeod, Ltd., 1974.

<u>Contents</u>: (W. W. Norton & Co., edition)

<u>Encounter in April</u> (1930-1937)
First Snow, p. 19.
"She Shall be Called Woman," p. 20.
Strangers, p. 27.

<u>Inner Landscape</u> (1936-1938)
Prayer before Work, p. 31.
Architectural Image, p. 32.
Understatement, p. 33.
Summary, p. 34.
Address to the Heart, p. 35.
Memory of Swans, p. 36.

<u>The Lion and the Rose</u> (1938-1948)

To the Living, p. 91.
The Tortured, p. 95.
The Birthday, p. 96.

The Leaves of the Tree (1948-1950)
Myth, p. 99.
Song without Music, p. 100.
The Swans, p. 101.
The Second Spring, p. 102.
Kot's House, p. 103.
To an Honest Friend, p. 104.
Landscape Pursued by a Cloud, p. 105.
Evening Music, p. 106.
Lullaby, p. 107.
Islands and Wells, p. 108.
Boy by the Waterfall, p. 109.
Poets and the Rain, p. 110.
Winter Grace, p. 112.

Land of Silence (1950-1953)
The First Autumn, p. 116.
The Sacred Wood, p. 116.
Summer Music, p. 117.
As Does New Hampshire, p. 118.
Transition, p. 119.
Villanelle for Fireworks, p. 120.
Provence, p. 121.
Journey by Train, p. 122.
Evening in France, p. 123.
From All Our Journeys, p. 124.
Where Warriors Stood, p. 126.
Take Anguish for Companion, p. 127.
Innumerable Friend, p. 128.
The Caged Bird, p. 130.
The Land of Silence, p. 131.
Letter to an Indian Friend, p. 132.
Of Prayer, p. 133.
The Tree, p. 135.
A Light Left On, p. 136.
Because What I Want Most Is Permanence, p. 137.
Song: "This is the love I bring," p. 138.
Leaves before the Wind, p. 139.
In a Dry Land, p. 140.
Prothalamion, p. 141.
Kinds of Wind, p. 142.
The Seas of Wheat, p. 143.
These Images Remain:

The Other Place, p. 189.
Definition, p. 190.
Forethought, p. 191.
A Pair of Hands, p. 192.
My Father's Death, p. 193.
The Light Years, p. 194.
Spring Day, p. 195.
By Moonlight, p. 196.
Reflections in a Double Mirror, p. 197.
Death and the Lovers, p. 198.

Cloud, Stone, Sun, Vine (1958-1961)
A Divorce of Lovers:
Now these two warring halves are to be parted/ p. 201.
I shall not see the end of this unweaving/ p. 201.
One death's true death, and that is--not to care/ p. 201.
I woke once out of a disturbing dream:/ p. 202.
Did you achieve this with a simple word? / p. 202.
What price serenity these cruel days? / p. 202.
Dear fellow-sufferer, dear cruelty, / p. 203.
Your greatness withers when it shuts out grief/ p. 203.
Now we have lost the heartways and the word, / p. 203.
What if a homing pigeon lost its home, / p. 204.
So drive back hating Love and loving Hate/ p. 204.
It does not mean that we shall find the place/ p. 205.
Others have cherished, perhaps loved me more;/ p. 205.
Wild seas, wild seas, and the gulls veering close;/ p. 206.
For all the loving words and difficult/ p. 206.
As I look out on the long swell of fields/ p. 206.
The cat sleeps on my desk in the pale sun;/ p. 207.
After a night of driving rain, the skies/ p. 207.
These riches burst from every barren tree;/ p. 208.
Where do I go? Nowhere, And who am I/ p. 208.
Now silence, silence, silence, and within it/ p. 208.
Out to the distant stars above this ground, / p. 209.
Moving In, p. 210.
Reflections by a Fire, p. 211.
Mud Season, p. 213.
Spring Planting, p. 214.
A Flower-Arranging Summer, p. 215.

For steadfast flame wood must be seasoned/ p. 389.
February Days, p. 390.
Note to a Photographer, p. 391.
March in New England, p. 392.
Composition, p. 393.
Burial, p. 394.
Of Grief, p. 395.
Prisoner at a Desk, p. 397.
Birthday Present, p. 398.
Elegy for Louise Bogan, p. 399.
Letters to a Psychiatrist:
Christmas Letter, 1970, p. 400.
The Fear of Angels, p. 402.
The Action of Therapy, p. 403.
I Speak of Change, p. 408.
Easter, 1971, p. 409.
The Contemplation of Wisdom, p. 409.

NOVELS

THE SINGLE HOUND

Boston: Houghton Mifflin Co., 1938.
Toronto: Thomas Allen, 1938.
London: Cresset, 1938.
Toronto: George J. McLeod, Ltd., 1948.

May Sarton's first published novel is the story of two poets: Doro, an elderly Belgian woman writer known to the literary world as Jean Latour; and Mark Taylor, a young Englishman whose emotions are stirred by Latour's poetry. It is almost inevitable that the two eventually come together, especially since Mark, recognizing this strong emotional attraction to Latour's writing, feels an overwhelming desire to meet and talk with her. But before this meeting he encounters Georgia Manning, a married artist, and briefly shares a passionate, intense love affair with her. When the affair ends he realizes that physical passion, although fulfilling and rewarding, cannot fully satisfy his emotional needs. This satisfaction comes when he is finally able to meet Jean Latour (as Doro) and they share a strong emotional/intellectual bond, uniting both their minds and spirits in a communion of ideas.

THE BRIDGE OF YEARS

New York: Doubleday & Co., 1946.
New York: W. W. Norton & Co., 1971.

May Sarton's second novel is a chronicle of the years from 1919 to 1940 as they passed over the lives of the Belgian family, the Duchesnes. War is the thread which runs through this chronicle; the remembrance of World War I and its impact on the country and particularly its impact on this family and their loved ones; and the threat of World War II as it overshadows their feelings and attitudes. Paul Duchesne is a philosopher/writer; Melanie, his wife and the mother of three children, is also a business woman in Brussels. It is she who remains the strength and foundation for her children and husband as the pattern of their lives, their successes and defeats, are played out in the years between the destructiveness of two world wars.

SHADOW OF A MAN

New York: Rinehart & Co., 1950.
Toronto: Clarke, Irwin & Co., Ltd., 1950.
Toronto: Ambassador Books, 1952.
London: Cresset Press, 1952.

Francis Chabrier, a twenty-six-year-old Bostonian, encounters several problems in this novel: his mother's recent death; his dual allegiance to a half French, half American heritage; and his apparent inability to "fall in love" with the young woman who loves him. In an attempt to sort out some of these problems, or to escape from them he goes to Paris. While there, he becomes involved romantically with an older Frenchwoman who helps him recognize his strengths and weaknesses and to accept himself and those who love him.

A SHOWER OF SUMMER DAYS

New York: Rinehart & Co., Inc., 1952.
Toronto: Clarke, Irwin & Co., Ltd., 1952.
London: Hutchinson & Hutchinson, 1954.
New York: W. W. Norton & Co., Inc., 1970.

Dene's Court, a great Irish country house, is the main "character" in this novel. Inhabited for the first time in thirty years by Violet Gordon and her husband upon their return from Burma, Dene's Court shapes the attitudes and behavior of all who inhabit it. Sally, the daughter of Violet's sister, arrives from America to visit the Gordons and gradually becomes intimately bound to this great house, to Violet and her uncle through a mesh of memories and remembered passions.

FAITHFUL ARE THE WOUNDS

New York: Rinehart & Co., Inc., 1955.
Toronto: Clarke, Irwin & Co., Ltd., 1955.
London: Gollancz, 1955.
New York: W. W. Norton & Co., Inc., 1972.

The story is partly based on the death by suicide of a professor of American literature at Harvard University. Sarton's character, Edward Cavan, is shy and seemingly remote from ordinary life, but is loved by his friends and respected universally for his knowledge and learning. Yet, the real Cavan was never understood; his deep political commitments were only tolerated by his colleagues. They were not aware of his need to be something more than "a witness" to life and, in the end, most of them never really understood why he died. His death sets off a wave of soul-searching among all those who had any connection with him and, in one way or another, their lives are changed.

THE BIRTH OF A GRANDFATHER
New York: Rinehart & Co., Inc., 1957.
Toronto: Clarke, Irwin & Co., Ltd., 1957.
London: Gollancz, 1958.

In this chronicle about the Wyeths, a well-to-do New England family, Sarton explores the problems the characters confront in their relationships with each other and their attempts to communicate their feelings. The central figures are Frances and Sprig Wyeth, but past generations and younger Wyeths play important roles as well in the over-all development of the novel. With the birth of his grandson, and the death of his closest friend, Sprig slowly begins to understand himself in relation to Frances, and in the end, he begins to arrive at the capacity to meet his wife on her own emotional ground.

*THE FUR PERSON (Illustrations by Barbara Knox)
New York: Rinehart & Co., Inc., 1957.
Toronto: Clarke, Irwin & Co., Ltd., 1957.
London: Muller, 1957.
New York: W. W. Norton & Co., Inc., 1968.
New York: New American Library, Inc., 1973 (paperback)

This is the saga of Tom Jones, a gentleman cat, whose decision to find just the right home proves successful after discovering the surroundings of "gruff voice." By giving up his ramblings as a "cat about town" he gains the love, care and affection of two people who respect his need for independence.

---

*A shorter version of this story appears in <u>All Cats Go to Heaven</u>. Beth Brown, comp., New York: Grosset & Dunlap, 1960, pp. 397-403.

THE SMALL ROOM

New York: W. W. Norton & Co., 1961.
Toronto: George J. McLeod, Ltd., 1962.
London: Gollancz, 1962.
New York: Norton Library, 1976 (p.b.).

The main theme of The Small Room is the question of the "price of excellence." Taking place on the campus of a New England women's college, the plot evolves around a student's act of dishonesty and how it eventually involves the entire student body and faculty, finally bringing into question the relationship of teacher to student. Lucy Winter, a new teacher, is confronted with this question of excellence when she discovers the plagiarism of Jane Seaman, a prize student of Carryl Cope. A dynamic, demanding teacher who expects nothing short of excellence from her students, Cope is forced to re-examine and re-evaluate her expectations, both of her students, her fellow teachers and of herself when confronted with Jane's plagiarism. Through the clashes that erupt over this incident, Lucy Winter learns "... only to the extent that a teacher commits her whole self can she expect from the student a like commitment, and insure the learning process."

JOANNA AND ULYSSES (Illustrations by James J. Spanfeller)

New York: W. W. Norton & Co., 1963.
Toronto: George J. McLeod, Ltd., 1963.
London: John Murray Publishers, Ltd., 1963. (Illustrations by David Knight)
Glasgow: Blackie & Sons, Ltd., 1967. (Introduction and notes by Vincent Whitcombe)

This small book is a "tale" describing the friendship of Joanna, a discouraged young Athenian artist, with Ulysses, a donkey she saves from cruelty and neglect. Just beginning a month's well-earned holiday, Joanna rescues Ulysses, but through her act of kindness she threatens to ruin her chance of enjoying the solitude she hoped for. Eventually, this minor "threat" fades as Ulysses becomes a symbol for her own inner person, one who had been neglected and rejected too. By nursing Ulysses back to health and happiness, Joanna brings herself back to life as well.

MRS. STEVENS HEARS THE MERMAIDS SINGING

New York: W. W. Norton & Co., 1965.
London: Peter Owen, 1966.

Toronto: George J. McLeod, 1966.

This unusual novel explores the source(s) and nature of poetic inspiration. Seventy-year-old Hilary Stevens, a poet of renown, prepares herself to meet the probing questions of two young interviewers from a national magazine. During the course of their afternoon visit, Hilary searches her past as it has crystallized in a series of flashbacks which uncover the "provenance" of her poetic inspiration which has always been feminine. The character of Mar, a young man confused about his homosexuality who seeks out Hilary's critical advice about his rough poetic outpourings, complements her reminiscences and gradual awareness of the nature of her own Muse.

MISS PICKTHORN AND MR. HARE: A FABLE

New York: W. W. Norton & Co., 1966. (Illustrated by James Spanfeller)

Toronto: George J. McLeod, Ltd., 1966.

London: Dent & Sons, 1968.

Miss Jane Pickthorn, a retired schoolteacher who has retained a love for translating Horace, "... tries to dislodge Trumball Hare who has moved into the run-down house across the way from her." She is offended by his way of life but discovers, only after he is gone, that Hare had been "living inside poetry." If she had allowed herself to "translate" him she would have recognized that "It is not the possessor of many things whom you will rightly call happy. The name of the happy man is claimed more justly by him who has learned the art wisely to use what the gods give."

THE POET AND THE DONKEY

New York: W. W. Norton & Co., 1969. (Illustrated by Stefan Martin)

Toronto: George J. McLeod, Ltd., 1969.

The central figures in this story are an aging poet, Andy Lightfoot, and an aging donkey whom Andy "borrows" for the summer from a neighbor. The poet is sorrowful because he has lost his inspiration and the donkey is stiff with arthritis. But when the two come together for solace they learn to know and understand each other. Love and care are the restoratives that help them overcome their sense of loneliness and emprisonment.

KINDS OF LOVE

New York: W. W. Norton & Co., 1970.

Toronto: George J. McLeod, Ltd., 1970.
New York: Avon Books, 1972. (Paperback edition)

The story is set in Willard, a small New Hampshire town which is often visited over the years by "summer people." Christine and Cornelius Chapman, elderly and long-standing summer people, retreat to Willard following Cornelius' stroke, resolving to live there during the winter months. During these long days and nights the Chapmans learn the wild and gentle secrets of this untamable town and come to know a rich variety of people who live different kinds of love, passion and courage.

AS WE ARE NOW

New York: W. W. Norton & Co., 1973.
Toronto: George J. McLeod, Ltd., 1973.

This novel is written in the form of a diary, kept by Caroline Spencer, a retired mathematics teacher. Unable physically to fully care for herself, her relatives decide to place her in a "rest home." While there she and the other elderly people are subjected to subtle humiliations and petty and unthinking cruelties. Caroline fights back to preserve her dignity, identity and sanity, but in the end, sees only one way to "overcome" the lonely horror of neglect.

PUNCH'S SECRET

New York: Harper & Row, 1974. (Illustrated by Howard Knott. A children's book for the ages four to eight.)
Toronto: Fitzhenry & Whiteside, Ltd., 1974.

Punch's secret comes in the form of a little mouse with "... tiny hands and a white breast and beautiful ears." She has come to his cage after dark to share his seeds and at long last Punch's loneliness vanishes as he realizes "... at night it is good to be loved."

CRUCIAL CONVERSATIONS

New York: W. W. Norton & Co., 1975.
Toronto: George J. McLeod, 1975.
London: Gollancz, 1976.

Crucial Conversations concerns the break-up of a marriage as seen through the eyes of Philip, a family friend who has been deeply involved in it and becomes torn between his love for both parties. Fifty-year-old Poppy Whitelaw, wife and sculptor, decides to abandon her long-term marriage to Reed. The more she grows as an individual, the more confining her marriage becomes. She cannot tolerate her husband's patronizing attitude toward her serious desire to be an artist, while he cannot understand why the expensive studio he built for her did not satisfy her needs. In the middle of these misunderstandings, Philip tries to help with his emotional support for both Poppy and Reed, but the break comes in spite of his efforts. For Poppy, the only resolution is to dissolve her marriage and discard the confining expectations of both family and friends. In the end, she is on her own, scared but free.

A WALK THROUGH THE WOODS

New York: Harper & Row, 1976. (Illustrated by Kazue Mitzumura)

Toronto: Fitzhenry and Whiteside, Ltd., 1976.

In this, her second children's book, Sarton extends an invitation to the reader to join the poet for a special walk through wild, beautiful woods with her dog Tamas and her cat Bramble.

We are each absorbed
in looking
and listening
and smelling
the spring smells,
woodsy and mossy
and wet.

NON-FICTION

I KNEW A PHOENIX: SKETCHES FOR AN AUTOBIOGRAPHY
New York: Holt, Rinehart & Winston, Inc., 1959.
Toronto: Clarke, Irwin & Co., Ltd., 1959.
London: Peter Owen, 1963.
New York: W. W. Norton & Co., Inc., 1969.

This is a book of autobiographical fragments consisting of early memories of Sarton's Belgian childhood; of her scientist/historian father, George Sarton, and her mother Mabel; her experiences at Shady Hill School in Massachusetts; a theatrical apprenticeship with Eva le Gallienne's Repertory Theater in New York; and her eventual initiation and experience as a writer. Portions of this book appeared (in somewhat different form) in The New Yorker. See Essays and Articles, p. 38.

PLANT DREAMING DEEP
New York: W. W. Norton & Co., Inc., 1968.
Toronto: George J. McLeod, Ltd., 1968.

In this autobiographical chronicle of May Sarton's renovation of an old house and farm in New Hampshire, she writes of her passion for gardening, her need for solitude and of the challenges she meets with the changing seasons. She probes the secrets of her home and grows to meet the demands, "seasoned and stretched to plant her dreaming deep."

JOURNAL OF A SOLITUDE
New York: W. W. Norton & Co., Inc., 1973.
Toronto: George J. McLeod, Ltd., 1973.

This work is a diary of Sarton's daily life, her fears, rages, anger and despair as well as her wild joy and ecstasy, great peace and solitude. She wrote this journal to balance the effects of Plant Dreaming Deep in which only the benign nature of her personality was revealed. By keeping this daily record, Sarton writes, "... I hope to break through into the rough, rocky depths, to the matrix itself."

A WORLD OF LIGHT: PORTRAITS AND CELEBRATIONS
New York: W. W. Norton, 1976.

In this autobiographical work Sarton celebrates the "great friendships that flowered" during her late adolescence and on into middle age. These are posthumous portraits of individuals who, in one way or another, influenced Sarton's life and who still remain alive in her memory.

ESSAYS AND ARTICLES

"Copeau in Florence: Modern Theatre in a Corral," Theatre Arts Monthly. 19 (September, 1935), 656-658.

In this essay Sarton writes of the French director Jacques Copeau, who has visited Florence to direct Alessi's Savonarola for the Maggio Musicale Fiorentino (May Festival). Describing his magnitude, she notes that this Frenchman, who speaks no Italian, changes, by his fire and verve, a milling, noisy crowd of actors into people of the 15th century, "... intent, fierce, passionate and beautiful." "... slowly from the hearts of the people themselves the magnificence grows of this play written and produced for the glory of the city of Florence."

"Story of Genius," Saturday Review of Literature. 20 (June 2, 1939), 11.

Sarton, reviewing Kathleen Coyle's book Immortal Ease, describes the work as readable, the material provocative and illuminated by understanding and technical virtuosity, but, from the point of view of literature, it is "disappointing." The novel is about a poet, Victoria Rising, whose character suggests Elinor Wylie. Rising is presented as a beautiful, sensitive woman, but by some flaw in her nature, she is driven to flee every major experience in her life. Sarton believes that instead of fleeing into the difficult solitariness from which she must write, Rising ends up ceasing to exist. Coyle's story does not add to our understanding of poetic genius, "... and I can see no other reason for writing a book about a poet than to do this."

"The Stern Growth of a Lyric Poet," The University Review (University of Kansas City). 6 (October, 1939), 68-70.

Sarton writes that the growth of the lyric poet is not as easy one. The art of the lyric is deceiving because it appears to have been written without any effort. "Actually nowhere is the struggle more complex, more difficult, more compact than in these small perfections." Yeats is a perfect example, according to Sarton, of the measure of "intensity of thought," in his life and in his work. His Autobiography is the anatomy of his growth as a poet," a growth that took him out of active Irish politics and into the world of myth and fantasy." By the stubborn intensity of his thought, Yeats had mastered his talent by the time he reached later years.

"Introduction," The Poets Speak: Twelve Poems from a Series of Readings at the New York Public Library. New York: New York Public Library, 1943, p. 5.

This poetry reading was an experiment by the library, "... in the hopes of further opening the ways of communication between those who read and those who write." Even though the poems read may seem unrelated, Sarton notes, they represent the works of poets who vary in their approach both to the form and the content of poetry. For this reason, they give an intimation of the richness and variety of the almost unlimited range of poetry today.

"Benelux: Belgium," Town and Country, September, 1947, pp. 112-113, 131.

Post-war Belgium is described as a "holiday country" for the war-weary tourists who arrive to enjoy the food, drink and peaceful "richness" of the land. The city of Brussels is the mecca of those in Europe who want to experience a still civilized capital. But, Belgium is not all charm; there are still scars. War collaborators from the days of the German occupation are resented; staples such as bread, butter and sugar are rationed and very expensive; rents are high and coal is scarce. Even the King is suspect and is to be investigated for his activities during the five year occupation. Even in the light of freedom and liberation, Belgium's prosperity depends on that of her neighbors; the economic stability of France and England are essential to her own life.

"Benelux: Netherlands," Town and Country, September, 1947, pp. 113-114, 188, 191-192.

On a trip through the Netherlands Sarton describes her reactions to the beauty of both the people and the land. Their heritage of dress, Delft earthenware and fabric, combined with the immaculateness of the houses and streets all contribute to an impression of peace. "... we carried back with us an impression of ... stability, work, and something I can only call health. The little villages we passed were decorated with hundreds of tiny orange flags (colors of the House of Orange) and as we rode by them in the gathering twilight, we too wanted to put out flags and to shout, 'Up with the Orange! Long live Holland!'."

"Forward," Beloit Poetry Journal. 1 (Fall, 1950), 3-5.

As an editor for this particular issue of Beloit Poetry Journal, Sarton defines where she stands, as a poet and as a critic: "... absolute statements about poetry make me angry." "By taking sides poetry is being endangered. A literate person who cares for poetry should recognize ... many kinds of poetry as having value." For Sarton's own poetry she has developed a "deceptive clarity" rather than obscurity; an "intellectual tension" rather than vagueness. But, for her choice of other's poetry in this edition, she has included, in some cases, "baroque imagery." Finally, she writes, "But one thing all these poets and poems did have for me, the power to seize my imagination and take me into themselves."

"Those Who Stay Away," Episcopal Church News, February 3, 1952, pp. 20-21.

In this essay Sarton explores the disparity between her need to satisfy a spiritual longing and the failure of organized religion to fulfill this longing. She asks: "What is it that I do not find in the churches which I do find in the theologians Simone Weil, Augustine, or Kierkegaard on the one hand, and in nature and moments of silent attention on the other?" Churchgoing for Sarton has been an unpleasant, unsatisfying experience, on the whole, because the sense of personal communion is absent. At the same time, trying to be fair, Sarton suggests that possibly her lack of patience and willingness to attend church regularly has kept her from experiencing those rare moments when, "... through the ritual itself and one's true awareness of its meaning, the presence of God is vividly present." But, she sees the problem as also a lack on the part of the church and the minister to recognize the real spiritual needs of individuals. "We are all, those outside, as well as those inside the church, far readier than churches have recognized for the full impact, for the challenge, for the Cross. We are in great need of feeling and recognizing within us the power of love."

*"In My Father's House," New Yorker. 29 (January 9, 1954), 29-31.

Sarton describes the "way of living" in her paternal grandfather's house in which George Sarton, her father, was reared. George Sarton's mother died shortly after his birth, and consequently he was "pampered and neglected by the maids" and grew up in an essentially lonely surrounding. But, there were some moments of intimacy between him and his father that saved the young boy from total isolation.

"O My America," New Yorker. 29 (February 6, 1954), 26-28.

Sarton recounts her initial impression of America when, in 1915, she and her mother left Europe to join George Sarton in the United States. Her intimates included a golden St. Bernard named Teddy, and Dick, the chauffeur. Later, the wife of the Sarton's host became an important influence on May. She describes her as so American but so Belgian, "... the perfect bridge from my own Belgian to American." The Sarton's finally settled in Cambridge where George Sarton worked on his life-long project, the Introduction to the History of Science, while teaching at Harvard University.

"Wondelgem, the House in the Country," New Yorker. 29 (January 23, 1954), 32-34.

In this essay Sarton describes the country house in Belgium where she was born in 1912. She was too young to personally remember much of the house but it was lovingly evoked in many of her mother's recollections. It was in this house that her mother gardened and created designs in wood and cloth. It was also in this house that her father launched his review, Isis, devoted to the history of science and civilization. But their happy life here was not to last; in the wake of the advancing German army the Sartons fled to England and finally to America. For May, the memories of this house begin and end on one day in 1919 when she re-visited there, meeting with an overgrown

---

*The following seven essays from the New Yorker appeared, in somewhat different form, in Sarton's book I Knew a Phoenix.

garden and a house defiled and dirty from war-time occupation. All but a Venetian glass, some plates and her father's notes were destroyed. But, the atmosphere of the house never died because it was so full of life and radiance.

"I Knew a Phoenix in My Youth," New Yorker. 30 (April 3, 1954), 29-33.

Sarton remembers her early days at the Shady Hill School in Cambridge, Massachusetts as being disciplined and rugged, but, rich and exciting as well. Agnes Hocking was the head school mistress but taught poetry as well; it was she who influenced May Sarton in the art of reading and writing poetry. "She did not tell us about poetry; she made us live its life." "Poetry was not something told, it was something happening to us."

"A Wild Green Place," New Yorker. 30 (August 28, 1954), 24-29.

In this essay Sarton describes her mother's early childhood experiences on a farm in Wales. She was sent to the farm to live while her father and mother traveled on business. It was in this surrounding of a wild, green country that the little Mabel Elwes was to be given "the gift of solitude." Her stay was a long period of solitary communion with nature and was a preparation for much that was to happen later. Even though she lived with two women, the older Grannie, and her younger, moody daughter, "... much of her day was spent alone, away from human contact." Sarton, musing about her mother's early experiences with loneliness and solitude, believes it was a "... time full of secret riches, which she understood because she was already the person she was to become, able to face reality and to face it with ... courage, on her own terms."

"Titi," New Yorker. 30 (September 11, 1954), 110-119.

The Institut Belge de Culture Française, a school Sarton attended when she was twelve, consisted of a faculty of two women: Marie Closset, known in the French and Belgian literary world as Jean Dominique; and Marie Caspar, known to the young pupils as Titi. Sarton describes Titi as a "... small angular figure, with a face extremely fine and sensitive in repose. But it was seldom in repose." Titi taught every subject and was constantly a force in the pupil's lives. Although she was feared, she was also adored, partly because of her "fantastic sense of humor." During this period the presence of Marie Closset was sensed and felt because her personality "created an atmosphere of awe," but Titi, with her tantrums and her love, was a very real person to the students. She "... had the ability to make us feel that we were not only her pupils but her dearest friends, as well, ..."

"Marc the Vigneron," New Yorker. 30 (January 8, 1955), 28-31.

Marc Turian, a long-time friend of Sarton, owned and operated a small, independent Swiss vineyard. In the Swiss economy the wine industry suffered from the importation of French, Spanish and Italian wines, and unfortunately the smaller, Swiss vignerons suffered the consequences. Yet, in the face of economic problems, Marc continued to produce wine, seeking for that perfect vintage. Sarton describes her friend as a "... great oak of a man with an inner life rich in fantasy." "He takes on the aspect of a legend for me ... because he is like a final explosion of individuality and character under circumstances that will soon no longer exist."

"The Novelist and His Characters," Writer. 68 (October, 1955), 335-337.

Rather than relying on autobiographical character, Sarton writes, the writer should completely imagine and create his/her own character. Imagined characters grow from the subconscious, triggered perhaps by the memory of a face. In this essay Sarton insists that the character must be able to stand on his/her own and not be manipulated by the writer. As a summary, she tells the aspiring writer not to be afraid of the power to create. "The deep layers of memory are more authentic than conscious copying from life." Also, be flexible enough to allow the character some independence, and don't be disturbed if he/she becomes so alive as to change the design of the novel. Finally, be flexible but don't lose sight of the theme.

"Shield of Irony," Nation. 182 (April 14, 1956), 314-316.

May Sarton is critical of those who would insist that irony should become one of the canons of literary appraisal. "In a period of timid retreat from the avant-garde positions taken by our forebears ... the novel is lapsing into long-winded particularized realism; neither conviction or passion are much in the atmosphere." "To the novelist and poet of today, alienated and neurotic irony is used as a shield. It permits him to adopt the prevailing attitudes without committing himself. In poetry the use of irony made possible the incorporation of ... ambivalence, under the guise of honesty." Sarton believes that American writers must commit themselves to the humanity within themselves before they can earn the right to irony, "... and irony may once again become a sword, rather than the final self-defense of the smug and uncompassionate."

"Good-by to a World," Reporter. 14 (April 19, 1956), 39-43.
Subtitled "Memories of Being 19 in Paris," Sarton describes her stay in this city (without her parents) when she was supposed to be studying the theater and absorbing the culture and arts surrounding her, but instead, lived in a drafty ground floor apartment while spending her days wandering the city, casual and solitary. "I did nothing wise or sensible," she writes, but she does remember this period as one of the happiest in her life; it was a time of freedom--freedom to sit and do nothing if she pleased, or freedom to listen to music, talk with friends, or just sit alone and think.

"Through the Skin," Nation. 183 (August 18, 1956), 145.
In her review of Richard Church's Over the Bridge, Sarton comments: "One writes autobiography because by pouring over the pool of childhood slowly coming to see again the lost treasure on the floor of the mind, we recapture not innocence but revelation, and so come to discover who we are." "The evocation of Proust lifts this book to its special grace."

"In Memoriam," Bruxelles: Presses de W. Godenne, 1957. (This essay written in French, was loosely translated by Dr. Charles Paul, Professor of Humanities, San Jose State University, 1975.)
May Sarton wrote this essay in memory of Raymond Limbosch, a Belgian poet and writer. Re-examining his work she views it as a "longue inquietude" (long anxiety) held in balance with a moving courage; a long search to refine not only the form of French poetry

but to reform himself.

> ... une longue recherche non seulement pour affiner la forme de la poésie française, mais 'la réforme de soi-même,' (Valery)

Examining specific works by Limbosch, Sarton reflects upon a question he frequently puzzled over, why one becomes a poet, ("Pourquoi devient-on poete?") In essence, his response was one becomes a poet because of the compulsion to answer the great questions that gnaw at you and the need to be delivered from the tension by song, i.e. lyric poetry.

> On le devient, il me semble, si d'abord les grandes questions que se pose toute être humain vous rongent, vous dévorent et vous brûlent au point que vous vous sentiez forcé de les extérioriser pour mieux les soutenir d'abord; et puis, si souffrant d'une tension extrême, vous êtes en même temps délivré par le moyen du chant: ...

"Sukiyaki on the Kona Coast," Reporter. 16 (June 27, 1957), 37-39.

In this piece Sarton vividly describes her visit to an island in Hawaii: "On this evening we felt the enchantment of the peril of living on the island volcano, born in fire, flowering and slowly dying in an illimitable relentless blue of sea and sky." Later she describes a small, out-of-the-way "restaurant" in which she and friend were surprised and delighted to enjoy a delicious sukiyaki meal, carefully prepared by a Japanese family. Talking with the owner of this small, isolated place and witnessing the closeness of the family with their surroundings Sarton appreciated the moment of intimacy she was able to share with that which will probably never be again.

"The Failure of the Dream," Education Summary, October 5, 1957, p. 5.

Sarton directs her attention to a discussion of the values of our society and how they affect, often times in a negative way, the younger generation. This is especially true in America where material things have become all important to so many people. Yet, America does offer one the opportunity to "realize" one's own dream, if only one is brave and courageous enough to have worthwhile dreams. Sarton believes that America's young people crave responsibility, work and discipline but since adults treat them like children long after they have "grown up," they unfortunately shun these values later in life. She contends that these same young people realize that if they do not have to work for something, they will not appreciate its value. Quoting Yeats' idea, 'In responsibilities begin dreams,' Sarton believes that everyone, in order to realize a dream, must work hard to understand and master the reality of it.

"The Writing of a Poem," Scripps College Bulletin. 31:2, 1957, 17 pages.

"The Writing of poetry is first of all a way of life, and only secondarily a means of expression." "It is a life discipline in which the poet must be aware and attuned to the world around him." Defining poetry as a "... collision between a state of awareness ... and an object ..." she believes it to be the "... perpetual reincarnation of the spirit through a concrete image...." After the awareness comes the transference, from the emotion to the communication by means of a created poem. This transference is a part of a transference from feeling to thinking. Sarton stresses the importance of the poet's ability to think in images: "Poetry is a way of life as well as a complex and fascinating intellectual game."

"A Poet Looks at the Learning Process," Shady Hill News, February, 1959, pp. 2-4.

In this selection Sarton discusses the learning process through a series of poems she has written over the years. These poems deal, in one way or another, with teaching and learning. She admits that she has learned more by teaching because, "... one begins to learn when one begins to be wholly committed." The poems included are: "For a Teacher of Mathematics: Ruth Edgett"; "The Sacred Order"; "Before Teaching"; "Dialogue"; and portions of "To the Living."

"Some Home Thoughts from Abroad," New York Herald Tribune/ Book Review, August 23, 1959, p. 2.

Re-visiting the house in Belgium celebrated in her earlier novel, Bridge of Years, May Sarton recognizes that her feelings are different: "... I have changed, for now I have a home of my own and part of me is still in Nelson, New Hampshire." "I know that I have at last become an American, since I can claim five fireplaces, a long open meadow, some steep woods that tangle their way down to a brook." At one point in her life Sarton felt that possibly Europe meant the lyric impulse and America those studies in relationships which demand the sustained creation of writing novels. But, like the countries, both disciplines are important for her. "I have never doubted that what I hope to say before I die requires both mediums and that my work must be considered as a whole."

"The School of Babylon," The Moment of Poetry. Don Cameron Allen, ed., Baltimore: The Johns Hopkins Press, 1962.

This is an important essay in which Sarton discusses the theme of "tension in equilibrium," both in the poem and in the poet. For the poet one of the permanent tensions is between the public and the private person. In the poem, the tension may be "... between the past and the present, the idea and the image, the music and the meaning, the particular and the universal, the creator and the critic or the silence and the words." "A poem emerges when a tension that has been something experienced, ... releases a kind of anxious striving about of words and images ..." Finally, Sarton writes, "... in poetry, as in painting, at the point of highest tension lies also the point of supreme release."

"On Living in a New England Village," Country Beautiful. 1 (1961), 26-30.

May Sarton describes her village of Nelson, New Hampshire, as "... the metaphor that has come to mean for me the adventure of solitude." Upon first seeing the village she was struck by the silence, and through the months which followed, it was the silence that enfolded and freed her at the same time. Even though an isolated area, there is an invisible web that unites the neighbors in the village; they do not intrude in each other's lives but in time of trouble, this web is drawn tight.

"Poet's Letter to a Beginner," Writer. 75 (April, 1962), 19-21. (This essay also appeared in The Writer's Handbook. A. S. Burack, ed. Boston: The Writer, Inc., 1968, pp. 396-401; pp. 383-388, 1975 ed.)

"An important quality for the poet, even before any actual writing, is to 'think in images'...." "The poet's mind desires the specific and the concrete." To Sarton, rhyme is the least important element in a poem; "... the shape and weight and tone of the poem as a whole are important." To develop one's own poetic voice one must be familiar with the poets of the past, both distant and immediate. "The actual writing of a poem is the process by which the poet thinks his or her feelings out." But the work does not stop there; revision is a necessary step, and an exciting one, because, "... by means of it the poet comes to understand more about the experience of the poem itself."

"Books with a Lasting Effect," Rocky Mountain News, April 11, 1962.

After an initial encounter at sixteen with Ibsen's The Master Builder, Sarton later "discovered" Virginia Woolf, becoming greatly influenced by her novel To a Lighthouse. Isak Dinesen's Out of Africa, read much later, has somewhat the same effect on Sarton as Woolf: "... the meeting with a compassion and imagination necessary to understand and communicate the inner life of a woman." The poetry of Yeats and the prose of Thoreau, and later, Simone Weil's Gravity and Grace and Martin Buber's Between Man and Man made significant impact on her life. Sarton views these works, and others such as the poetry of George Herbert and the novels of Jane Austen as bound together in the sense that "... in each we meet an exceptional human being who has fashioned a personal style out of the necessity to communicate a vision of life."

"An Informal Portrait of George Sarton," Texas Quarterly. 5 (Autumn, 1962), 101-112.

Describing George Sarton as an "... exceedingly charming man who moved with propulsive energy ..." May Sarton writes of her father as a "... crusader in a war to convince the universities and the academics that the history of science must be treated as a separate discipline." Sarton recounts her father's growing disillusionment with Harvard for what he believed to be a state in which his time and talents were being used without recompense, or very little recompense. After twenty years of work he was finally awarded a professorship and an honorary doctorate but his unhappiness with the university remained. "George

Sarton reached out, not only toward scholars in the field but toward all men and women of good will. He may have been criticized by some for being sentimental and self-dramatic, but he reached a wider public than scholars usually do and will be remembered for his humanity and keenness for life."

"The Design of a Novel," Scripps College Bulletin. 37, 1963, 15 pages.

According to Sarton the novel is concerned with the interrelation of several "... psyches and their impact on each other." Theme and character determine plot; the plot is only what has to happen because certain characters are set down in certain situations. Theme, defined as the "haunting question the writer hopes to answer," quickens, but plot can often kill. Overall, the design of a novel is an organized process, according to Sarton. The writer must allow the novel to stand on its own--the writer must recognize what is relevant even when it appears to change the design. "Writing a novel is a long, involved process in which the writer, as well as the reader, must be changed, must grow."

"Revision as Creation," The English Leaflet. 64 (1965), 3-7.

Indefinite revision, Sarton contends, is necessary for the poet for two reasons: to facilitate a deepening of the poet's understanding of what he really means; and, to develop an organic structure by which the meaning can be communicated. "The image helps the poet explore by means of revision; the music of the idea compels change." Sarton emphasizes the relationship between form and the intensity of the experience; the greater the intensity behind the poem, the more complex and tight the form must be. Free verse, although not shunned by Sarton, is not indiscriminately used because it often leads to unclear thoughts and sloppy expression.

"A Garland of Neighbors," Country Beautiful. 4 (1965), 30-35.

May Sarton lovingly describes the neighbors who were a part of her life in Nelson, New Hampshire; Quig, a man who made and played violins and painted with oils. "Did anyone sit down and talk with Quig who did not feel more alive when he left than when he came in? His magic was his humanity." The Warners, a close knit family of parents, children and animals. Grace Warner was the strong matriarch of this loving family who thrived off the land they loved; Perley Cole, the retired farmer who helped May Sarton keep her landscape in shape, working at it as a game and only when the spirit moved him. "... I knew when I came here that I had found a house where I could work in peace, but I never dreamed that it would bring me in touch with so many rich lives, a tonic for the values I cherish most; the free spirit, fiery courage, humor and the power to endure."

"On Growth and Change," The Christian Science Monitor, March 16, 1966, p. 3.

The poet in middle age, Sarton contends, can go on growing if he learns to remain transparent. Up to this time in her poetic career Sarton had written mainly formal, structured verse because she believed it satisfied her need for the absolute. But, with the publication of A Private Mythology, some of the poems were beginning to move away from traditional verse forms. She felt that her poem "At Lindos" represented a breakthrough from structured verse to free verse. This new (for her) poetry helped her to appreciate her poetry as a way of "opening out, a horizon."

"Problems and Delights of Revision," Writer. 79 (December, 1966), 20-22.

"Revision of a poem is going forward into the highly complex ... process of creation." In analyzing an emotion or thought in terms of its poetic possibilities, the poet must ask, "... has (it) come to me in the form of a single strong metaphor?" The poet can test the strength of a metaphor by revising it. To test the whole poem the poet must consider the words and phrases, keeping to the concrete. He must also consider the forces, shape, tone of voice and mood, metre, and rhyme. "Revision helps the poet bring the poem closer to its own reality."

"Revision as Creation: The Growth of a Poem," The CEA Critic. 29 (June, 1967), 1, 3.

"Revision is creation." "The writer earns form as he earns understanding. Metaphor is the teacher of the poet, and a fusion of intellect and emotion for the reader who meets and understands the poem." Sarton discusses how the idea for a poem grows out of a struggle, question or conflict that must be resolved. The image, by probing and analyzing, becomes a concrete idea. After this initial state of inspiration, the poet begins the "act of creation," a conscious act of critical probing and analysis. "The art of poetry will demand the capacity to break down over and over what has already been created, and break down barriers within the poet's self so that he may keep on growing within the whole form and shape of life."

"For the Once and Future Child," New York Times Book Review, May 5, 1968, pp. 6, 42.

Of the twelve children's books May Sarton reviews in this article, she found only two to be "absolute treasures:" W. S. Gilbert's A Song to Sing, O!, illustrated by Rosemary Wells, and Edward Lear's The Jumblies, impressively illustrated by Edward Gorey. In reviewing these books, Sarton writes, "What more delightful bundle to find in the big white mailbox on the village green in mud season than a pack of children's classics? Books to nibble at, meditate upon, sometimes greet with a burst of laughter or, at times, with the furious attention of the once and future child as one sits in the big wing chair by the fire, absorbed in recaptured and new found joys."

"Homeward," Family Circle Magazine, June, 1968-June, 1969. The cover title "Homeward" consists of the following series of twelve monthly articles May Sarton wrote for the Family Circle Magazine:

"Riches Beyond Measure," Family Circle Magazine, June, 1968, p. 8.

"In June we are safe in a green and flowery world." In June Sarton rises with the sun because "... so much is happening outdoors." The birds are feeding their young, the iris is ready to bloom and the subtle morning sunlight begins to melt the dew. Even after the first freshness has gone she glories in the growth and change the garden experiences as the day grows. "It has to be caught on the wing, like all the best things in life. It would be fatal to hold them back--June, or the early morning, or youth or love as it grows and changes."

"A Quiet Summer Night," Family Circle Magazine, July, 1968, p. 4.

Country dwellers become used to the "usual sounds" of the rural landscape such as chattering birds or mice scratching at night. But, Sarton admits, occasionally there are startling noises like thunder or wood snapping in the cold. On one particular summer night Sarton was awakened by what she thought were "... low insistent conspiratorial voices in the ... meadow," but quickly realized they were only bullfrogs "conversing" in a distant pond. Before she could return to sleep there came the sound of excited barking from a pack of dogs. Angry that they might be chasing a young deer, she dressed and ran out with her rifle to scare them away. Tramping through the bushes, she failed to locate the dogs and became lost and confused. Much later, very tired, she returned home, only to be startled again by a clanging crash. Her investigation led to the discovery of a fat racoon robbing the garbage can. "Country silence is wonderful--but I have to get home to it, sometimes, through some pretty strange noises."

"Old Home Day," Family Circle Magazine, August, 1968, p. 10.

Old Home Day is celebrated every August in Nelson, New Hampshire, and becomes an opportunity for reunion and renewal of family and friends. The whole town prepares for this day by cleaning, painting, mending and generally renovating their surroundings. The day itself is casual and informal with picnics, games, music and guest speakers. One year Sarton was asked to be the speaker, and for her presentation she chose to read some poems from a small volume of verse she had gathered for the occasion. "... by the end of the twenty minutes I felt the silence of communion and consent. It was a strange and unforgettable experience to be there, part of what I had described in the poems themselves, no longer an outsider looking on...."

"The Mowing, Before and After," Family Circle Magazine, September, 1968, p. 76.

Sarton describes the annual mowing of her hayfields and the varied feelings it inspires as she watches the horses and men work together in harmony at this ancient ritual. Since she has no grazing animals, her neighbors, the Warners, mow the hay and store it in her barn for their own livestock. "The Warners do more than work hard; they keep alive for us here in the village the poetry and skill of farmers of fifty years ago." After the mowing, the once grassy field, scattered with rocks and wildflowers, becomes a long green lawn. "It is like a poem when all the extra adjectives have been pruned out, lean and clean and making a plain strong statement."

"Memorable Gifts," Family Circle Magazine, October, 1968, pp. 33, 101.

"The best gifts are works of imagination. They come with the giver's signature on them, wrapped in a personal magic, and that is why we treasure them." Among the gifts Sarton treasures are a milk-weed pod, "... just as it burst open ... trapped in a clear plastic paperweight...," and an album of photographs of her house and village, taken, developed, enlarged and printed by a friend. Even "purchased" gifts can have meaning if the giver personalizes them. Preparing for the coming Christmas season Sarton writes: "We can bring back the fresh glory of the Christmas Star ... by loving not only the people to whom we give but the gift itself...."

"The Silent Ones," Family Circle Magazine, November, 1968, n. p.

"We are silent people, my two cats and I." "None of us has said a word, but in our silence there is communion." Sarton loves her cats; "... they are wild and secret and lead their own lives." If she goes away for more than a day the cats become "alienated"; they may not show their affection for several hours after her return. "But, after awhile they return to their usual silent, purring selves, sometimes playful, most of the time silent presences."

"A Country Christmas," Family Circle Magazine, December, 1968, pp. 20, 24.

May Sarton and a close friend, celebrating the Christmas season together in Nelson, hoped to "... recapture the simple Christmas of a childhood and to make it ours again." A mantel laden with cards and messages from friends and a tree decorated with ornaments collected over a period of twenty years are exciting and exhilarating. On Christmas Eve, if the road is passable, they will go to the Warners' manger to symbolically remember that "Love came to us so humbly, born in a manger, with the sweet smell of hay, and the warm animal breath for welcome." "Animals keep our innocence alive."

"January Blues," Family Circle Magazine, January, 1969, n. p.

January, notes Sarton, a month of blizzards and bitter north wind, does not "... feel like the beginning of anything." But January is one of Sarton's best working months; the cold winds and snow close around the house like a mantle. Sitting in her study with a fire in the fireplace is like being in a "cocoon of silence, ..." "There is a joy of the timeless." January is without color except for the bulbs that bloom indoors on the window sills. Yet, all is not dead or silent. January is the new year--lambs are born "... in the dead of winter and come as a tiding of great joy."

"Valentines All Year Round," Family Circle Magazine, February, 1969.

The giving of a valentine present is spontaneous, a giving from one heart to another. "St. Valentine's Day summons us to create something special for those we love, but the truth is that we should send valentines all year round when the spirit moves us." "Tenderness itself contains true regard for the dignity and even the 'otherness' of the person to whom it is addressed." If St. Valentine's Day can keep tenderness alive, that is for the better; "... it is, perhaps, what keeps us human in the end."

"A Good Shepherd," Family Circle Magazine, March, 1969, p. 90.

In this article Sarton writes of her fourteen-year-old neighbor, Cathy French, who raises sheep as a serious business. Her father had originally given Cathy twin lambs when she was only five, but from this pair she learned to care for and raise many sheep. She sold both the wool and meat, earning enough money to buy her own horse. Sarton asked Cathy what it was about sheep that made all the hard work worth while, and she answered, "... I love them because they have a touch of loving...." Sarton writes, "A touch of loving is the key to the life on the French farm."

"Waiting for Phoebe," Family Circle Magazine, April, 1969, n. p.

"In April we watch and wait for the spring happenings--always perilous in this climate--to come off safely." Included in these "spring happenings" are chickadees in the pine trees, pussy willows, "... vivid coarse green and baroque shapes of the skunk cabbage," blue water in the lake, "bright-pink waxy flowers of the trailing arbutus," and, the phoebe, "... come home to refurbish the forlorn nest."

"Living with a Mountain," Family Circle Magazine, May, 1969, n. p.

The Grand Monadnock, a majestic and beneficent mountain, dominates Sarton's landscape near her home in New Hampshire. "The mountain appears and disappears with the changing seasons: in early spring it is often a clear intense blue; in summer it is hidden by a forest wall..."; in the fall, "... the broad flanks are copper, gold and crimson, with flashes of dark-green hemlock and pine"; and in winter its "bald summit" is white with snow. For Sarton, living with a mountain means being within range of its magnetic influence, not necessarily always with it. "So I am led to believe that intimacy does not necessarily imply 'never being out of sight' of the beloved object or person, for then we miss the intense joy of recognition when we have been away and come home."

"With Solitude for My Domain," Cornhill Magazine, Summer, 1968, pp. 419-425.

This selection is an excerpt from May Sarton's book Plant Dreaming Deep. She writes, "I had wanted air, light and space, and now I saw that they were exactly what the house had to give." Sarton describes her life and work in her house in New Hampshire, where writing, reading, gardening and thinking are an essential part of her days.

"Man from Another Time," Reader's Digest. 98 (June, 1971), 61-64.

Sarton pays tribute to her dear friend Perley Cole in this excerpt from Plant Dreaming Deep. She describes him as "... a man who came from another age, where a workman had the time and patience and the wish to do a perfect job...." Sarton had "hired" Perley Cole to help her with odd jobs around her property, little suspecting that this man in his seventies would carefully and patiently tame her wild landscape. "Gradually ... he trimmed out trees, enlarged the lawn and brought back the front green." Slowly, a friendship developed between this "untamed old man" and Sarton. After finishing work at noon they came together to share a glass of sherry and talk. "I have never heard him say anything that did not come from deep inside his own essentially solitary experience, and he has taught me a great deal." She believes that Perley Cole nourished her poetic soul by his pride and care in his own work. "There he is off in the woods cutting brush, and here I am at my desk pruning out a thicket of words. It's both companionable, in a curious, solitary way, and inspiring."

"Gardens Are a Demanding Joy," Vogue. 158 (August 15, 1971), 52-53.

May Sarton describes her first attempt at planting a garden after moving into her house in New Hampshire. Even before the planting takes place, there must be planning, a necessary process which takes forethought and contemplation. "Gardeners must have long thoughts, and perhaps that is why this demanding joy is a joy for the mature: the young do not plant trees." Sarton finds a relationship between the writing of a poem and the planting of a garden in that they both represent a "marriage between the formal and the wild." "One needs a fierce capacity for hard work, unlimited hope, and the allowance always of a wide margin for error or mischance when writing poetry or planting a garden." Yet, perfection, in writing poetry or gardening, will never be reached. "I sometimes think that we live most intensely by what we can fully imagine but never fully possess."

"The Leopard Land, Haniel and Alice Long's Santa Fe," Southwest Review, Winter, 1972, pp. 1-14.

"From the beginning Santa Fe was to be for me the place of poetry. I would go back over and over again, always in fear and trembling, as if to a source--." One of the overriding forces which drew Sarton to Santa Fe was in the personalities of Haniel and Alice Long, he an educator and poet, she a sensitive, perceptive woman. Sarton recounts their place in the Santa Fe landscape, their individuality and uniqueness, their rapport with the immensity of their surroundings, and their respect for the Indian and Spanish customs.

"One Life: Glory and Torture," Vogue. 161 (April, 1973), 63.
Reviewing Anne Morrow Lindbergh's Hour of Gold, Hour of Lead, Sarton believes that Lindbergh's greatness lies in her ability to maintain the polarity between her inner life and her well-known husband's activities. Awareness, vulnerability, discipline and courage are the source of her genius, according to Sarton. "Because it was necessary to remain reticent and often silent in the face of a public life, the discipline and censor worked toward a good kind of tension in her writing style and perhaps helped her to ... invent certain silences that run through all her work and make it breathe."

"Flower Watching," Vogue. 162 (August, 1973), 100.
"One truly sees flowers better when they are picked and brought indoors." By bringing them inside one is more aware of the poignance of their birth, life and death, all of which can take place in a few hours. Roses, Shirley poppies, English Bluebells and even water lilies are some of the flowers Sarton finds arresting and beautiful. "Flower watching is a consuming passion, with a touch of wisdom and a touch of madness in it."

"The Genius of Eva Le Galliene," Forum. 2 (Summer-Fall, 1973), 43-49.
To May Sarton, Eva Le Galliene communicates a "vision of life"; she has had profound influence on many people, in much the same way as a poet or composer does. Her genius is fashioned from within, "... it makes its own rules, creates its own 'image' and invents its own style." Her gift of interpretation as an actress is a form of criticism. Eva Le Galliene learned from Sarah Bernhardt and Eleonora Duse by giving passionate attention to their art. From Duse she gleaned "... the carefully concealed ...", from Bernhardt, the dramatic, theatrical gesture. Not only is she capable of ascertaining the tone, texture and rhythm of a play but her whole body and voice can communicate a tension and force. Her genius lies in her ability to project the soul itself, the "inwardness" of a human being.

"The Rewards of Living a Solitary Life," New York Times,

April 8, 1974, p. 35. (This essay also appeared in the following: Values and Voices: A College Reader. New York: Holt, Rinehart & Winston, 1975, p. 91; and To Be Alone (excerpt). Jane Austin, ed., New York: Crown Publishers, 1975, p. 82.)

"Solitude is the salt of personhood. It brings out the authentic flavor of every experience." "Loneliness is felt more sharply with other people because we suffer from our differences of taste, temperament and mood. With people the edge of perception is softened; one withdraws at the very instant of personal truth for fear of hurting...." For the most part, living a solitary life for Sarton has been a rewarding experience because it has allowed her to "converse" with her hidden powers.

"The Practice of Two Crafts," The Christian Science Monitor, June 25, 1974, p. F7.

"The art of the novel and the art of poetry are really at the opposite ends of a spectrum," Sarton believes, yet she has found it exhilarating to turn to the novel in the extended intervals when she could not produce poetry. She writes poetry and novels from different inner needs: in poetry she probes and searches for a metaphor to crystalize a feeling or idea; in the novel she consciously places certain elements in precipitation that will lead to the answer or answers of a difficult question. Ultimately, the poem is more satisfying to Sarton, "The novel is a dialogue with what is human, the poem a dialogue with a part of Creation itself." "The poem is close to 'The Ground of Being.'"

"The Magic Moment," House and Garden. 146 (December, 1974), 92-93, 175.

It is unfortunate that the Christmas celebration has become such a mixture of the sacred and the mundane that we become confused between them. Yet, there is always the magic moment when the rush and madness is forgotten and we find ourselves once again in the "childhood dream." For May Sarton this dream comes when the familiar ornaments are unwrapped: the "... English Father Christmas in his white and gold robe"; or a shiny blue ball that tinkles out Silent Night. "Christmas draws back to itself memories of a whole life." Sarton recalls a Christmas in Paris when she was only nineteen. She and two friends went to Chartres for midnight mass, feeling a great wonder and loneliness. Years later she recalls a midnight Mass in a small adobe church in Santa Fe. The Mass followed an Indian dance and ritual and "... all seemed woven together as if we were part of something mysterious and greater than any dogma." This mystery of renewal gives us Christmas again, "... in order that we can make a new beginning, to give of ourselves more deeply in the communion of saints on earth."

"Coming Home to New England," Ford Times. 68 (June, 1975), 3-5.

Even though not a "true" New Englander, Sarton writes of her love and admiration for this part of the United States. "New England grips the heart," she writes, partly because of its beauty and partly because of its ruggedness. "The answer to the magic of New England lies in the fact that all is contrast and sudden change within a sturdy framework." The people are tough, humorous and laconic, who, under their reserve, are "... highly emotional and steeped in natural wonders." One of the main reasons Sarton loves New England is the fact that the individual, even the eccentric, is cherished. "New England is and always has been a haven for free spirits, for those who are more interested in growth and change from within themselves than in ... changing the outside world."

"Notes from an Inner-Space Journal," Reader's Digest. 107 (August, 1975), 21-24.

This article, an excerpt from Sarton's book Journal of a Solitude, includes her thoughts on sex and love, the need to let the "psyche rest," people's demand for instant success rather than patient development of a craft, and the benefits that suffering has on one's personal growth.

SHORT STORIES

"Old Fashioned Snow," Collier's. 117 (March 23, 1946), 21.

A very short story of a young man who re-lives the joy and exhilaration of touching, feeling, tasting, smelling and becoming immersed in a powder white snowfall. He shares these feelings with his young nieces who build a snowman and enjoy the day with him in his white world.

"The Return of Corporal Greene," American Mercury. 62 (June, 1946), 691-695.

Ben Greene returns home from the war, uncertain of himself or his future. Before returning to his immediate family he decides to visit an aging cousin who had always welcomed and loved his visits, but when he reaches her house he learns from the gardener that she had died a month before. Too late, in anger and frustration, he realizes how much she had been a stabilizing force in his life while fighting a distressing and insane war.

"The Contest Winner," Liberty, August 10, 1946, pp. 22-23.

To occupy his time after retirement, Mr. Pepper takes to entering the many contests advertised in magazines and newspapers. He finds a great deal of satisfaction in figuring out ways to spend the hoped-for prize money; possibly a new car, a small farm in Vermont, a greenhouse. Molly, his wife, joins in these games of speculation, yet neither one really expects to win; it is just a game. One day, Mr. Pepper, much to his surprise, wins $1,000 and his pastime is no longer a game. He and Molly begin to argue over how the money should be spent, to the point where they both become disgusted and disillusioned. It is the arrival of a letter from Molly's sister which solves their problem. Confiding to Molly that her husband would be out of work due to an injury, it is only a moment before the Peppers' $1,000 is given to someone who really needs it.

"Mrs. Christiansen's Harvest," Ladies Home Journal. 64 (March, 1947), 72-73. (This story also appeared under the title "She Who Loved Flowers," in Ladies Journal (London), January, 1948, pp. 17-18.)

This is the story of Selma Christiansen, a strong-willed woman of Finnish background, who, year after year, determinedly plants and cares for a large flower garden. Her passion, even obsession, with the garden becomes "her pact against the death of the heart." Selma plants the flowers that her stern father, so many years before, had forbidden her to grow. It is only on her deathbed that Selma confesses to her husband the truth behind her driving need, even in failing health, to nurture her garden.

"The Town Will Talk," Ladies Home Journal. 64 (June, 1947), 72-73.

Lucinda Howarth and Nathaniel Sumter, two aging, strong-willed people, thrive on each other's crusty but loving arguments. One day they surprise everyone by deciding to marry. Even in the face of criticism from others, they recognize their need for each other's companionship.

"The Miracle in the Museum," Church and Home (London), March, 1948, pp. 22-23.

Caroline Santiago, arriving in New York from New Mexico, hopes to visit her son Tony who lies sick in a hospital. Unfortunately, the doctors suggest that she wait until the boy's crisis has passed. Wandering around a strange, chilly city is frightening and lonely so Caroline decides to take refuge in a warm lobby of an art museum. The exhibition is a comforting and familiar one to her when she recognizes the carved wooden figures made by sculptors from the early days of her New Mexico. In her innocence and faith Caroline kneels before the statue of a "thin Christ on the cross" to pray for her sick son. The curious people gather around to stare, some moved, others appalled at her superstitious beliefs, but when she returns again the next day, people are waiting for her, many recognizing their own lack of faith and compassion. When Caroline is finally allowed to visit Tony his crisis has passed, and his recovery a certainty. Her prayers in the museum have produced a miracle, not only for Tony, but for those who witnessed her unsophisticated and honest show of faith.

"The Paris Hat," illustrated by R. G. Harris, Cosmopolitan. 124 (March, 1948), 42, 150-154.

Because of a pink straw hat, Ellen Frazer's life takes on exciting and rich overtones. Arriving in Paris on a vacation, the quiet, reserved and somewhat frightened Ellen "discovers" a pink straw hat quite by chance. Wearing it transforms her from the drab, timid woman to the bright, lovely, young lady. The beauty had always been there but she had not recognized it. Her brief encounter with a wise old woman and, later, a young poet, reinforce her beauty. As the old woman had admonished her, "... one must first learn to love oneself before one becomes lovable," and Ellen learned to love that part of herself that the pink hat revealed.

"Mr. Pomeroy's Battle," Homes and Gardens, November, 1948, pp. 14-17, 64.

Mr. Pomeroy, a high school Latin teacher for the past twenty-five years, suddenly finds his position threatened by the innovations of a young, new principal. Latin must be dropped from the curriculum because it does not fit in with the progressive program, according to the principal. Mr. Pomeroy, much to his dismay, must teach algebra if he is to remain on the staff. To everyone's surprise, especially Mr. Pomeroy's, his first day in algebra class with the new freshman students evolves into a dissertation on the humanizing and civilizing qualities of Latin as a life study. The students, moved by his words, generate a call for the reinstatement of the subject and the principal finally agrees, accepting Mr. Pomeroy's conviction that "education has to do with values, not with subjects."

"If This Isn't Love," illustrated by Gwen Fremlin. Woman's Home Companion. 76 (April, 1949), 20-21, 96-98.

Sally, a young college woman, discovers the world of passion and emotion in her relationship with a new suitor. She does not know how to handle her feelings for this young man who, on the surface, appears to be in complete control of himself. Much to her surprise, he is as frightened and confused as she about these feelings. It is only after they share their uncertainties that their relationship matures.

"The Little Purse," illustrated by Donald Teague, Redbook,

June, 1949, pp. 33-35, 99.

For nine-year-old Molly, finding a purse heavy with coins seemed the answer to all her frustrations and unhappiness. She just knew that the money would help relieve some of the worry her parents were suffering. In Molly's mind it could provide them with all the material things they desired. But, when the contents are counted and there is only eighty-seven cents, Molly is crushed and disillusioned. She cries to her father, "... it was for you and Ma--to have everything--and now I can't do it--." This concern on the part of a little girl opens the parents' eyes to their own failings and gives them the courage to work and save together for their happiness.

"Alyosha and His Horse," World Review. 12 (September-February, 1949-1950), pp. 45-50, 77.

Alyosha, a White Russian with a proud past, now lives in poverty in a coastal village on the Mediterranean. At one time he had been a circus rider with the Cossack troupe and was famous for his triple somersault. Now, he doesn't even own a horse and has come to believe he is only half a man without one. Alyosha believes that his problem can be solved only if he can meet a rich woman who would buy him a horse. Much to his surprise he does meet a rich woman in Myrtle, but her reaction to his request is anything but receptive. A proud woman who is ever conscious of those who would "cultivate" her friendship simply to gain access to her money, Myrtle is unable to accept Alyosha as he is, a unique and different individual, willing to be honest about his needs. In the end, both are left impoverished. Alyosha admits, "She needs love as much as I need a horse. We are both beggars, but she has no horse to give me and I no love to give her."

"The Last Gardener," Woman's Day, April, 1953, p. 82.

While wishing for a gardener to help her with the yard, the aging Susan Hubbard is suddenly confronted with Monsieur Planteau. Old and lonely, but with stamina and verve, he admires her garden and asks to help her care for it. "I've been looking over this garden. It suits me," he said, "Like a man who has made up his mind to spend a fortune without a second thought." For a moment Susan is hesitant, but the old man's manner is so straightforward and his desire so sincere that she finds herself gradually helping him plan the planting. "It was going to be a fine day . . . a day for young lovers, but then Susan thought, an even better day for old gardeners."

"The Screen," Harper's Bazaar. 88 (October, 1953), 248, 254.
The screen in this story is a barrier of fear, anger and misunderstanding that Dexter Randall has unconsciously dropped between himself and his daughter. He sees so much of his overly-demanding wife in his daughter that Dexter finds himself treating both the girl and his wife the same. After Mrs. Randall suffers a nervous breakdown and is sent away to a hospital, he must confront his daughter alone. Treating the girl like an individual in her own right rather than a carbon-copy of his wife allows Dexter to drop the screen that had blocked a mutual love between father and daughter.

"Aunt Emily and Me," Woman's Day, April, 1960, pp. 36-37, 98-102.
Nine-year-old Daphne decides she would rather visit her great aunt for the summer than attend summer camp which she regards as a "hell where unwanted children are dumped." Before too long the eighty-year-old aunt and the nine-year-old girl experience a comradeship and affection that gives both a feeling of worth and satisfaction. It is with a feeling of relief that they realize they can share each other's company; so often in the past their individuality had caused others to misunderstand them.

"Joanna and Ulysses," Ladies Home Journal. 80 (September, 1963), 70-72, 86, 88-92, 94, 101.
This short story was also published as a book. See p. 32 for annotation.

POEMS NOT IN VOLUMES OF POETRY

ABSENCE OR PRESENCE
Virginia Quarterly Review. 42 (Summer, 1966), 403.

AFTER A SHOCK
Virginia Quarterly Review. 42 (Summer, 1966), 404.

AFTER ANGER
The Malahet Review, April, 1968, pp. 54-55.

AUTUMN SONNET
Falling Fountains. 1 (January, 1974). 15.

THE BEECH WOOD
Ladies Home Journal. 72 (October, 1955), 100.

BIRD OF GLASS
Atlantic Monthly. 166 (September, 1940), 364.

A BUNCH OF ROSES
Voices. 151 (May-August, 1953), 24.

CHRISTMAS, 1974
New York Times, December 24, 1974, p. 19.

A CHRISTMAS ELEGY
Yankee, December, 1968, p. 196.

COLD NIGHT
Virginia Quarterly Review. 42 (Summer, 1966), 403-404.

COLD SPRING
University Review. 8 (March, 1941), 176.

CONSTRAINED IT CAN BE. SHORT OF DEATH/
(From the sequence entitled "Over Troubled Water")
Francis Marion Review. 1 (1975), 14.

THE CONTEST
Ante, Summer, 1967, p. 62.

EASTER EGG
Saturday Review. 38 (April 9, 1955), 31.

ELEGY FOR A BLACK CAT
A Celebration of Cats. ed., Jean Burden. New York: Paul S. Eriksson, Inc., 1974, pp. 73-74.

ELEGY: FOR KATHLEEN FERRIER
Pennsylvania Literary Review. 8 (1957), 9.

ELEGY: THE POET LEAVES THE ACADEMY
Virginia Quarterly Review. 42 (Summer, 1966), 406-407.

EPIPHANY
Massachusetts Review. 1 (Summer, 1960), 719.

EVERYWHERE, IN MY GARDEN, IN MY THOUGHT/
(From the sequence entitled "Over Troubled Water")
Francis Marion Review. 1 (1975), 11.

THE FEBRUARY OWLS
Plume and Sword. 4 (May 4, 1964), 14.

FIRST LOVE
(From the sequence entitled "Words on the Wind")
Poetry. 97 (December, 1930), 144.

THE FOUNTAIN
Voices. 178 (May-August, 1962), 28-29.

FRUIT OF LONELINESS
(From the sequence entitled "Words on the Wind")
Poetry. 97 (December, 1930), 144.

THE GHOST
Pennsylvania Literary Review. 5 (1954), 17.

THE GHOST IN THE MACHINE
Transatlantic Review. 19 (Autumn, 1965), 71-72.

THE GIFT
New York Herald Tribune, November 21, 1952, p. 18.

THE GIFTS
Briarcliff Quarterly. 3 (April, 1946), 62-63.

HERE LET ME LIE QUIET UPON YOUR SHOULDER/
Atlantic Monthly. 183 (March, 1949), 59.

I SIT AT MY DESK IN A HUGE SILENCE/
(From the sequence entitled "Over Troubled Water")
Francis Marion Review. 1 (1975), 11.

IF YOU TAKE REFUGE IN A WORLD THEN BEAR/
(From the sequence entitled "Over Troubled Water")
Francis Marion Review. 1 (1975), 15.

IMAGE
London Mercury. 36 (September, 1937), 419.

ITALIAN VERSE
New Yorker. 29 (August 1, 1953), 53.

IT'S THE TIME OF BREAKING, YOUR HOUSE SOLD/
(From the sequence entitled "Over Troubled Water")
Francis Marion Review. 1 (1975), 16.

THE JUST EXCHANGES
The Husk. 29 (December, 1949), 49.

LAST NIGHT I STOOD BESIDE YOU IN YOUR HELL/
(From the sequence entitled "Over Troubled Water")
Francis Marion Review. 1 (1975), 15.

THE LEGEND HAUNTS US STILL, EACH OF US WEARS/
(From the sequence entitled "Over Troubled Water")
Francis Marion Review. 1 (1975), 14.

LET NO WIND COME
(From the sequence entitled "Words on the Wind")
Poetry. 97 (December, 1930), 145.

LETTERS TO MYSELF (Two poems)
Virginia Quarterly Review. 42 (Summer, 1966), 404-405.

LINCOLN MEMORIAL
New York Herald Tribune, February 10, 1949, p. 28.

LITERAL NOW, THE TREMBLING AND THE FEAR/
(From the sequence entitled "Over Troubled Water")
Francis Marion Review. 1 (1975), 12.

LOVE CANNOT ACT, AND SO I MUST EMBARK,/
(From the sequence entitled "Over Troubled Water")
Francis Marion Review. 1 (1975), 13.

NEVER IS SILENCE CRUEL, NO,/ (Variant reading)
Poetry. 74 (August, 1949), 272-273.

A NORTHERNER SEES THE COTTON FIELDS FOR THE FIRST TIME
(From the series entitled "American Notebook")
Poetry. 59 (February, 1942), 240-241.

O THAT I WERE AS GREAT AS IS MY GRIEF/
University Review. 12 (Spring, 1946), 214-215.

OF THE MUSE
Virginia Quarterly Review. 42 (Summer, 1966), 402.

OHIO COUNTRY
(From the series entitled "American Notebook")
Poetry. 59 (February, 1942), 239-240.

OVER TROUBLED WATER (13 sonnets)
Francis Marion Review. 1 (1975), 11-17.
I sit at my desk in a huge silence/ p. 11.
Everywhere, in my garden, in my thought/ p. 11.
Literal now, the trembling and the fear/ p. 12.
The poet dances on a rope held taut/ p. 12.
Love cannot act, and so I must embark,/ p. 13.
We know the legend of clear loving eyes/ p. 13.
The legend haunts us still. Each of us wears/ p. 14.
Constrained it can be. Short of death/ p. 14.
If you take refuge in a word then bear/ p. 15.
Last night I stood beside you in your hell,/ p. 15.
It's the time of breaking, your house sold,/ p. 16.
So there was, after all, no destination/ p. 16.
We got off where we started months ago/ p. 17.

PAVILION
Niagara Falls Gazette, June 15, 1940, p. 26.

THE POET DANCES ON A ROPE HELD TAUT/
(From the sequence entitled "Over Troubled Water")
Francis Marion Review. 1 (1975), 12.

THE PRIVATE PACE IS SCREAMING (AT ANY WRITER'S CONFERENCE)
Beloit Poetry Journal. 2 (Spring, 1952), 4.

SESTINA
(From the series "Three Poems")
Poetry. 65 (February, 1945), 231-233.

SILENCE IS NEVER CRUEL/ (Variant reading)
Poetry. 74 (August, 1949), 272-273.

SIMPLE FUGUE
Pennsylvania Literary Review. 8 (1957), 8.

SO THERE WAS, AFTER ALL, NO DESTINATION/
(From the sequence entitled "Over Troubled Water")
Francis Marion Review. 1 (1975), 16.

SONG FOR A MARRIAGE
Ladies Home Journal. 71 (August, 1954), 110.

SONNET: WHEN IN THE LIGHT-STORMED AND ARIEL CITY/
Virginia Quarterly Review. 35 (Summer, 1959), 410.
The Various Light. eds., Leah B. Drake and Charles Muses, Switzerland: Aurora Press, 1964, p. 305.

SPRING AIR
New York Herald Tribune, April 30, 1952, p. 18.

SPRING CHORUS
Choral Speaking in the English Course. comp., Cecile de Banke, Massachusetts: Walter H. Baker Co., 1943. pp. 44-47.

THE TEACHERS
Queen's Quarterly. 52 (Autumn, 1945), 279.
Ladies Home Journal. 70 (January, 1953), 66. (only three stanzas of the original five)

THEY ALSO
(From the series entitled "Words on the Wind")
Poetry. 97 (December, 1930), 145-146.

TO AN ANGEL
Beloit Poetry Journal. 1 (1951), 5-6.

THE TREE IN THE CLOUD
Ladies Home Journal. 67 (December, 1950), 167.

TROUBLE IN CAMBRIDGE
New Republic. 111 (August 28, 1944), 246.

TWO SICK KITTENS
Cat Fancy. 15 (November-December, 1972), 16.
A Celebration of Cats. ed., Jean Burden. New York: Paul Eriksson, Inc., 1974. p. 32.

VILLANELLE 1941 (WE MUST BE PERMITTED TO MOURN OUR DYING KIND)
Decision I. 5 (May, 1941), 43.

THE WATER MEADOWS
Ladies Home Journal. 68 (June, 1951), 150.

WE GOT OFF WHERE WE STARTED MONTHS AGO/
(From the sequence entitled "Over Troubled Water")
Francis Marion Review. 1 (1975), 13.

WE KNOW THE LEGEND OF CLEAR LOVING EYES/
(From the sequence entitled "Over Troubled Water")
Francis Marion Review. 1 (1975), 13.

WHERE THE GRASSES (EASTERN KANSAS)
(From the series entitled "American Notebook")
Poetry. 59 (February, 1942), 235-237.

WHERE THOUGHT LEAPS ON
Ladies Home Journal. 75 (February, 1958), 140.

WHILE THE GREAT MOON RISES
Ladies Home Journal. 68 (May, 1951), 231.

WINTER LIGHT
Pennsylvania Literary Review. 8 (1957), 7.

WORD FROM LIMBO
Virginia Quarterly Review. 42 (Summer, 1966), 407-409.

POEMS IN ANTHOLOGIES

America in Verse: A Treasury of Patriotic Poetry. comp., Donald T. Kauffman, New York: Pyramid Books, 1968.
"In Texas," pp. 77-78.

Anthology of Magazine Verse and Yearbook of American Poetry for 1938-1941. ed., Alan F. Pater, New York: The Paebar Co., 1942.
"Charleston Plantations (Drayton House, Middleton, Runnymede)," p. 412.
"In Texas," p. 413.
"An Old Song," p. 414.

The Best Poems of 1943. comp., Thomas Moult, New York: Harcourt, Brace & Co., 1944.
"Santos: New Mexico," pp. 53-54.
"Celebrations," pp. 69-71.

Best Poems of 1956. Stanford, Cal.: Stanford University Press, 1957.
"After Four Years," p. 79.

Best Poems of 1958. Palo Alto, Cal.: Pacific Books, 1960.
"Spring Planting," p. 88.

Best Poems of 1959. Palo Alto, Cal.: Pacific Books, 1961.
"A Field of Grain," p. 88.

Best Poems of 1960. Palo Alto, Cal.: Pacific Books, 1962.
"Franz a Goose," p. 105.

Best Poems of 1964. Palo Alto, Cal.: Pacific Books, 1965.
"At Lindos," p. 108.
"The House in Winter," p. 110.

A Celebration of Cats. ed., Jean Burden, New York: Paul Eriksson, Inc., 1974.
"Elegy for a Black Cat," pp. 73-74.

"Great Cats and the Bears," pp. 154-155.
"Tiger," p. 159.
"Two Sick Kittens," p. 32.

The Choice Is Always Ours. ed., Dorothy Phillips, New York: Pyramid Publishers, 1975.
"Santos: New Mexico," p. 123.

The Earth Is the Lord's: Poems of the Spirit. comp., Helen Plotz, New York: Thomas Y. Crowell Co., 1965.
"Santos: New Mexico," p. 116.

Enough of Dying! eds., Kay Boyle and Justine Van Gurday, New York: Dell Publishing Co., 1972.
"The Tortured," pp. 293-294.

Garlands for Christmas. ed., Chad Walsh, New York: Macmillan, 1965.
"Nativity," pp. 53-54.

The Golden Year. eds., Melville Crane, et al., New York: Books for Libraries Press, 1960.
"Conversation in Black and White," p. 239.

High Wedlock Then Be Honored. ed., Virginia Tufts, New York: Viking Press, 1970.
"Prothalamion," p. 279.

Imagination's Other Place. ed., Helen Plotz, New York: Thomas Y. Crowell, 1955.
"The Sacred Order (For George Sarton)," p. 155.

Modern Love Poems. ed., D. J. Klemer, New York: Doubleday & Co., 1961.
"By Moonlight," p. 78.
"Definition," p. 74.
"These Images Remain":
Now that the evening gathers up the day,/ p. 31.
Even such fervor must seek out an end,/ p. 31.
"Fore Thought," p. 89.
"In Time Like Air," p. 34.
"Leaves before the Wind," p. 21.
"A Light Left On," p. 66.

Modern Religious Poems. ed., Jacob Trapp, New York: Harper & Row Publishers, 1964.
"New Year Wishes," p. 251.

"Song: Now Let Us Honor with Violin and Flute," p. 175.
"The White-Haired Man," p. 173.
"The Work of Happiness," pp. 246-247.

New Coasts and Strange Harbors: Discovering Poems. comps., Helen Hill & Agnes Perkins, New York: Thomas Y. Crowell, 1974.
"Summer Music," p. 91.

New Poems by American Poets. ed., Rolfe Humphries, New York: Ballantine Books, 1953.
"Transition," p. 137.
"Summer Music," p. 134.
"Prothalamion," p. 135.
"Leaves before the Wind," p. 136.

New Poems by American Poets #2. ed., Rolfe Humphries, New York: Ballantine Books, 1957.
"A Celebration," p. 136-137.
"Nativity (Piero della Francesca)," p. 137.

New Treasury of War Poetry, The Poems of the Second World War. ed., George Herbert Clarke, New York: Houghton Mifflin Co., 1943.
"From Men Who Died Deluded," p. 131.
"Santos: New Mexico," pp. 213-214.

New World Writing 10. New York: The New American Library, 1956. (Translations by May Sarton)
"Life That Passes," Pierre Saghers, p. 99.
"The Voyages," Robert Sabatier, p. 100.

The New Yorker Book of Poems. New York: Viking Press, 1969.
"In Time Like Air," p. 343.

Pictures that Storm Inside My Head; Poems for the Inner You. ed., Richard Peck, New York: Avon Books, 1976.
"The Ballad of Ruby," p. 46.
"Girl with 'Cello," p. 133.

The Poetry of Railways. comp. K. Hopkins, London: L. Frewin, 1966.
"After a Train Journey," p. 103.

The Questing Spirit. eds., Halford Luccock and Frances Brentano, New York: Coward-McCann, Inc., 1947.
"Santos: New Mexico," p. 277.

Rising Tides: Twentieth Century American Women Poets. eds., Laura Chester and Sharon Barba, New York: Washington Square Press, 1973.
From "The Invocation to Kali," pp. 64-67.
Parts I, II, V.

A Time to Love. ed., Joan Berg Victor, New York: Crown Publishing Co., 1971.
"Definition," p. 79.

To Be Alone. ed., Joan Berg Victor, New York: Crown Publishing Co., 1974.
"Moving In," p. 24.
"After a Train Journey," p. 38.

Untune the Sky. comp., Helen Plotz, New York: Thomas Y. Crowell, 1957.
"The Clavichord," p. 18.

The Various Light. eds., Leah Bodine Drake and Charles A. Muses, Switzerland: Aurora Press, 1964.
"After Four Years," p. 303.
"Sonnet: When in the light-stormed and Ariel city/" p. 305.

Voices of Protest and Hope. comp., Elizabeth Dodds, New York: Friendship Press, 1965.
"To the Living," (excerpt) p. 139.

A Way of Knowing. comp., Gerald D. McDonald, New York: Thomas Y. Crowell, 1959.
"Innumerable Friend," pp. 186-187.

When Women Look at Men. eds., John Kouwenhoven and Janice Thaddeus, New York: Harper & Row, 1963.
"A Celebration (For George Sarton)," p. 240.

The Women Poets in English. ed., Ann Stanford, New York: Herder & Herder, 1973.
"At Lindos," pp. 258-259.

TRANSLATIONS

ALLUSION TO POETS (Odilon-Jean Perier)
Pennsylvania Literary Review. 4 (1955), 26.

*BATHER (Paul Valery)
Hudson Review. 12 (Spring, 1959), 92-93.

*BIRTH OF VENUS (Paul Valery)
Hudson Review. 12 (Spring, 1959), 92-93.

*CAESAR (Paul Valery)
Hudson Review. 12 (Spring, 1959), 92-93.

*CANTICLE OF THE COLUMNS (Paul Valery)
Poetry. 94 (April, 1959), 1-4.

THE DANCE OF THE FIRE (Robert Sabatier)
Literary Review. 4 (Spring, 1961), 361-362.

GIFTS (Francis Jammes)
Pennsylvania Literary Review. 4 (1955), 27.
In Time Like Air,† p. 76.

*IN SLEEPING BEAUTY'S WOODS (Paul Valery)
Hudson Review. 12 (Spring, 1959), 92-93.

LIFE THAT PASSES (Pierre Seghers)
New World Writing 10. New York: The New American Library, 1956, p. 99.
In Time Like Air,† p. 79.

PLAINTES (Louis Emis)
Literary Review. 4 (Spring, 1961), 333-334.

---

*Denotes those poems in which May Sarton and Louise Bogan collaborated on translation.

†May Sarton. In Time Like Air. New York: Rinehart & Co., 1958.

THE PRINCESS OF THE BLOOD (Robert Sabatier)
Literary Review. 4 (Spring, 1961), 361-362.

SONNET COMPOSED IN SOLITARY CONFINEMENT (Jean Cassou)
In Time Like Air,† p. 78.

*THE SPINNER (Paul Valery)
Poetry. 94 (April, 1959), 4-5.

THE STAR OF FROST (Louis Emis)
Literary Review. 4 (Spring, 1961), 333-334.

THIS PEASANT'S SON (Francis Jammes)
Pennsylvania Literary Review. 4 (1955), 27.
In Time Like Air,† p. 77.

*TO THE PLANE TREE (Paul Valery)
Poetry. 94 (April, 1959), 5-7.

THE VOYAGES (Robert Sabatier)
New World Writing 10. New York: The New American Library, 1956, p. 100.
In Time Like Air,† p. 80.

THE WATER CARRIERS (Robert Sabatier)
Literary Review. 4 (Spring, 1961), 361-362.

MISCELLANEA

FILM

A Better Tomorrow: Progressive Education in New York City. Documentary. Office of War Information, 1945.
The script for this film was written by May Sarton and Irving Jacoby.

The Valley of the Tennessee: The Story of the TVA. Documentary. Office of War Information, 1945.
The script for this documentary was written by May Sarton.

Hymn of the Nation. 1946.
Script by May Sarton, directed by Alexander Hammid. It was produced and edited for the Office of War Information by Irving Lerner and released by Arthur Mayer and Joseph Burstyn, Inc. The production featured Arturo Toscanini and the NBC Symphony Orchestra with Jan Peerce as soloist with the Westminster Choir. There appears a brief reference to the performance in the New York Times, April 22, 1946, p. 26.

PLAYS

The Underground River: A Play in Three Acts. New York: Play Club Inc., 1947.
This play was published but never produced.

The Music Box Bird: A Play in Three Acts.
This is an unpublished play, written, according to May Sarton, around 1962.

RECORDINGS

Woodberry Poetry Room/Lamont Library, Harvard College.

On four separate occasions May Sarton recorded readings of her poetry on master tapes or records:

(T 851.1/1) Tape, no date:
Sounds
The Clavichord
Oh, Who Can Tell?
The Second Spring
The Stone Resists
Now I Become Myself

(D 13.3/2,3,4) 4 78 RPM Discs, August 6, 1941.
Monticello
In Texas
Definition
Afternoon on Washington Street
From Men Who Died Deluded
Memory of Swans
Canticle #11
Architectural Image
Colorado Mountains
Of the Seasons
Santos: New Mexico

(T 830.9/2) Tape, March 26, 1951.
from: To the Living
The Dying
Santos: New Mexico
from: In Memorian
Letter to an Indian Friend
Second Spring
Now Voyager
The Window
Afternoon on Washington Street
These Pure Arches

(D 868.1/9) 33 RPM Disc, October 10, 1962.
Proteus
Franz, a Goose
A Village Tale
The Swans
Homage to Flanders
A Celebration for George Sarton
After Four Years
On Being Given Time
The Frog
The Furies
Binding the Dragon

At Muzot
The Light Years
Death and Lovers
Der Abschied
Reflections by a Fire: On Moving into an Old House in New Hampshire
On a Winter Night

Archive of Recorded Poetry and Literature. Washington, D. C.: United States Library of Congress, 1961.

This recording was made January 20, 1961, and contains the following sixteen poems:

Prayer Before Work
At the Bottom of the Green Field She Lies
Where Dream Begins
At Muzot
The Frog, That Naked Creature
The Phoenix
Homage to Flanders
Provence
Of the Seasons
Green Song
The Lady and the Unicorn
The Furies
A Celebration
Italian Garden
On Being Given Time
On a Winter Night

LETTERS AND MANUSCRIPTS

Amherst College (major collection: May Sarton's letters to Louise Bogan)

Boston University Muger Memorial Library

Harvard University, Houghton Library (major collection)

New York Public Library, Berg Collection. (The major collection)

Scripps College

Tulane University

University of Buffalo, New York. Poetry Collection,

Lockwood Memorial Library

Yale University

PART II:

WORKS ABOUT MAY SARTON

ENCOUNTER IN APRIL, 1937

Benét, William Rose. "The Phoenix Nest," Saturday Review of Literature. 15 (March 27, 1937), 18.

Benét is generally complimentary of Sarton's first volume of published poetry. Of the poem "First Snow" he writes that it possesses "aristocratic grace," but "She Shall Be Called Woman" is praised above all the other selections. Benét, in a critical comment, expresses a hope that Sarton's future work will be free of clichés, uncertainties and influences.

Conrad, Sherman. "First Discoveries," Poetry. 50 (July, 1937), 229-231.

A great many of Sarton's poems are sonnets, some very good, but, according to Conrad, she employs pre-fabricated emotions in order to achieve high polish. The poems seem to stem from literary rather than personal emotions. In addition, they recall, too often, the poetry of Edna St. Vincent Millay. Her free verse seems more effective. "She Shall Be Called Woman," according to Conrad, is the best poem in the volume; it represents that "... secret access that women have into the core of their sensations and feelings. From that heightened consciousness their best and unique work always comes."

Holmes, John. "Happy Isles," New York Herald/Books, June 6, 1937, p. 10.

The critic notes, "May Sarton ... makes the mistake of taking too many romantic short cuts to achievement." Further, the poem "She Shall Be Called Woman" degenerates to trite sentimentality. But the title poem is regarded as one worth reading because of its shrewd comment upon character.

________. "Poetry Now," Boston Transcript, May 15, 1937, p. 5.

Holmes writes that this book of poems exhibits a "... distinctly feminine sort of poetry." There is a "... delicacy and light color, a sense of the dramatic, a clear flash of emotion...." Holmes believes Sarton to be most effective in her sonnets, especially in her ability to work with the octet and sestet. But, she is least effective in her imitation of oriental verse.

Keller, Martha. Philadelphia Inquirer, July 10, 1937, p. 12.
The critic believes that Sarton's work is a little on the overesthetic and academic side, and obviously influenced by H. D. and Elinor Wylie, but her technique is sure and when she writes from experience "... her promise is amazing."

Leach, Henry Goddard. "Poetry Parade," Forum. 97 (May, 1937), 320.
The critic views the book as "... fragile, bitter, ... work of a New England girl for whom the cruder passions are refined into the fleeting shadows of angel wings."

"Lyric Love," Newark Evening News, March 4, 1937, p. 12.
Sarton's Encounter in April invokes comparison with Edna St. Vincent Millay, but ... "charming, graceful and melodious as her verses are, they lack Millay's gift of startling phrase and of impudence that manages to remain poetry." The most successful of Sarton's efforts is the poem "She Shall Be Called Woman" in which her free verse combines "candor with artistic skill."

"May Sarton's Volume of Free Verse and Sonnets," Springfield Republican, April 18, 1937, p. 7e.
Sarton's verse, "... rather sophisticated in thought, has a frequently pleasing command of images" notes this critic. She is at her best when writing in conventional Shakespearian sonnet pattern, such as the fifteen poems near the end of the book. Overall, the critic regards this volume as an attractively printed work of poems.

Poetry Review. 29 (January/February, 1938), 58-59.
A brief review in which the critic writes, "Gifted with the temperament of the artist, and possessing a sensitive and romantic vocabulary, the volume glows

with the evidence that here is a poet." ... "Emotion and perfection of form are to be found in this collection."

Tilghman, Teneh. Baltimore Evening Sun, May 8, 1937, p. 6.
The critic notes that this book is a technically creditable performance. She handles words and rhythms with skill, but the reader cannot escape the feeling that he has read all this before. "Miss Sarton follows too closely the formula made familiar by women poets of the Millay-Wylie generation, and the formula is now becoming a little thread bare."

Walton, Eda Lou. "The Poems of May Sarton," New York Times/Book Review, May 16, 1937, p. 24.
Walton believes this book has all the freshness and vitality--all the zest of youthful emotions, but it has little else. Her imagery is lush and rather overly plentiful; her sonnets are rough in technique but now and then she brings one off with success. "The aliveness of this volume is promising but she has not yet grown selective, nor has she achieved complete mastery of her medium."

INNER LANDSCAPE, 1939

Abercrombie, Ralph. "Poetry," Time and Tide, April 22, 1939, p. 514.
Speaking of Sarton's poems Abercrombie writes, "I believe they are unsuccessful; she aims at a precise vision, but does not achieve it because she does not use words precisely. She can command a great deal of metric skill, of a rather unadventurous type, ... it too often obstructs rather than crystallizes her intense (but incoherent) emotion."

De Selincourt, Basil. "The Blessing of Augury," The Observer (London), April 2, 1939, p. 5.
"If her verse deserves notice, it is because the intense experience which underlies and unifies them has engendered an uncompromising determination to forge and refine the tool for its expression, a tool which is ... deep-searching to the point of ruthlessness, and very delicate." Sarton's universality is wholly personal, according to this critic. Her poems must be read together to be understood for they tell the story

of "... human passion, unique, holy and unforgettable."

Hartley, Leslie. The Sketch, August 2, 1939, p. 236.
Hartley believes that Sarton's ideal is "... to free imagery of emotion." He sees her images as passing through "the frigidair of her mind, coming out crystalized and abstract to a fault." Yet, her perfect sincerity commands one's admiration, and, her use of language "... attains the sharp edge and precision of utterances." Sarton has originality and an austere artistic conscience.

Hawkins, Desmond. "Mr. Spender and Others," Spectator, May 19, 1939, p. 868.
According to Hawkins, Sarton's poems remain in the raw state, as ideas for poems. "Her language is trite and she is content with vague approximations to the meaning. Finally, there is too much padding with rhymes that make no sense."

Holmes, John. "Books," Boston Evening Transcript, March 1, 1939, p. 13.
With the publication of her second book of poetry, "May Sarton," writes this critic, "has grown not only wiser and stronger, but poetically more skillful." "Sarton writes of the inner world of love and loneliness and self-assurance, with its flat stretches, its peaks and dark nights and noons." Holmes praises the "Winter Landscape" poems, especially "Afternoon on Washington Street," and he sees "A Letter to James Stephens" as one of her more surprising and enjoyable poems. "... this book is a passionately real record of life, of inner life and a woman who has found herself...."

Hutchison, Percy. "The Butterfly Imprisoned in Ice," New York Times Book Review, March 15, 1939, p. 5.
"Sarton's poems are ordered on the surface but passionate beneath the surface. She uses words more often to conceal than to reveal. Her lyrics do not always tease the imagination of the reader enough that he is carried beyond the limits of the poem itself." "More color seems to be the needed ingredient for her lines."

"Introspective Verse," Christian Science Monitor, April 8, 1939, p. 8.
"Miss Sarton ... gives us a highly introspective

and accordingly somewhat monotonous collection too narrowed in interest to seem much more than words." This critic views Sarton's words as beautiful but too analytical to strike a warm response in the heart of the average reader.

Leach, Henry G. "Poetry of Distinction," Forum. 101 (April, 1939), 240.

In this brief review Leach notes that the poems in this volume reveal a further development of "... delicate intensity and restrained but exalted perception."

"May Sarton's Poems: A Second Collection, 'Inner Landscape'," Springfield Republican, April 30, 1939, p. 7e.

With these poems, the critic notes, "... there is the same touch of sophistication and the same delicacy of expression that characterized Encounter in April. The poem 'Letter to James Stephens' is a summarization of Sarton's philosophy of poetry."

Powell, Charles. "American Poet," Manchester Guardian, May 19, 1939, p. 7.

"It is a passionate verse, a verse of passionate thought and passionate feeling, with that fusion of the two which gives it its imaginative quality and control." Sarton's mastery of the sonnet form, writes Powell, yields strength and beauty. "Originality, intensity and urgency are qualities manifest in this volume of poetry."

Stephens, James. "A New Poet's Success," Times (London) April 16, 1939, p. 9.

Stephens writes, "The Author is in love with discrepancies for she adores love itself, and as equally loves that polar purity we call snow." "Sarton is able to do a thing hitherto impossible--she can warm snow, and regard it and love with a passion that makes them equally lovely. All this is done with an eagerness, a precision, which mark her talent as one of the notable of our present writers."

"Three Poets," Saturday Review of Literature. 20 (August 26, 1939), 17.

According to this critic Sarton's writing is flat, her diction usual, and most of all, "... there is a disregard of the implication of metaphor, a failure to perceive that figures may work at more than one level and that a surface effect is worse than useless if contradictory forces are contriving absurdity beneath the surface." Focusing on a line from the poem "The Vanquished," which reads, "Do not think for an instant that I will bear your pity/Across my mouth like a soft January rain,", the critic comments, "The facial intrusion spoils what might otherwise have been a respectable image." ... "Inner Landscape is a disappointing performance."

Times Literary Supplement, May 27, 1939, p. 318.
"Although Sarton's dominant theme is a human heart, a human passion and her mode intimately feminine, she submits both to the control of 'impassioned reason' and her verse is as intensely formed as it is felt." The critic notes her style is simple but sometimes too consciously cultivated. "Her verse suggests comparison with that of Elinor Wylie or Edna St. Vincent Millay and certainly does not suffer by it."

W. G. V. K. "Sarton's Dignified Lyrics," Boston Herald, March 18, 1939, p. 6.
"May Sarton's Inner Landscape is a bitterly and insistently personal book of poems. The subject is the poet's struggle to bring spiritual stability and strength out of ... an unhappy love affair." But, Sarton is aware of the dangers of "... bewailing lost love in print ..." and emphasizes her determination to be strengthened through the loss. "It is evidence of the author's considerable poetic ability that dignity is attained in so many of these poems."

THE LION AND THE ROSE, 1948

Bacon, Martha. "Marvels of Interwoven Syllables," Saturday Review of Literature. 31 (April 17, 1948), 50.
"We have a young woman poet of past achievement both in verse and in the novel who has now 'found herself' in a book of rare delight and unusual depths." Bacon sees Sarton as an artist of remarkable powers. "She makes use of simple combinations of words--and of the words of common speech--and has achieved a vocabulary and style distinctly her own. Sarton has not substituted correct ideas and enlightened opinions for a creative talent. Lion and the Rose is an achievement of the first quality."

Booklist and Subscription Books Bulletin. 44 (April 1, 1948), 266.

A short review in which the poems are regarded as pleasing, competent lyrics on various themes, including a section of love poems, and one on American places.

Jackson, Joseph Henry. "Books," San Francisco Chronicle/The World, June 13, 1948, p. 18.

"Sarton is always a sensitive, skilled writer--a bit too generous to herself, often reluctant to forgo the urge to elaborate an immediate poem out of something that might serve better as a facet or function of a deferred poem."

Kirkus Review. 16 (January 1, 1948), 44.

"Miss Sarton's work is marked by a kind of delicate passion, which often makes up for a certain weakness of technique...." "Like so many women poets, her poems are not held together by any ordered continuity of thought, but the individual poems are spontaneous and finely wrought."

McCarthy, Francis. "Flaws in the Poetry," New York Times Book Review, August 15, 1948, p. 18.

"Miss Sarton's poetry is most successful when its content is religious and its method most parsimonious. Her craftsmanship is scrupulous and deft but her conception of poetry lends itself too readily to didacticism." ... "The inward life is Sarton's primary theme; religion, humanism and democracy are beliefs movingly conveyed in 'Celebrations' and 'Return to Chartres.' McCarthy notes that some of her later poems lack the tension found in these.

Rosenthal, M. L. "The Mysterious Art of Singing Words," New York Herald Tribune/Weekly Book Review, July 4, 1948, p. 6.

"Almost the entire range of Sarton's verse is 'open country'." "Her lyric talent shows up best in the love poems, especially the sensual 'Magnet'." Rosenthal notes that she is one of the few modern poets influenced, in the right way, by Yeats. She retains an independent poetic personality in many of the poems in this volume. Only in a few poems, such as "Places of Learning," "The Work of Happiness," and

"Navigator" is there a hint of "sentimental dilution."

Smith, Ray. Permanent Fires: Reviews of Poetry, 1958-1973. Metuchen, New Jersey: Scarecrow Press, 1975.

Of the poems from "Theme and Variation" Smith writes that they attain a pure and rare diction. "Their ... symbolic language, which carries a conviction of condensed experience, is the best of the collection." Later Sarton abandons this and the personal urgency which gives it tension. "... she is perhaps above all a limner, and I believe that her least successful work comes when she strays outside the bounds of the gift...."

________. "The Rose and the Oration," Poetry. 63 (February, 1949), 292-293.

According to Smith the opening poems in "Theme and Variation" attain a diction "pure and rare." According to his interpretation, the lion symbolizes past experience; the rose the final form of experience, the poet's artifact. "For Sarton the alchemic translation that makes these poems so effective is the conviction of condensed experience." ... "When she abandons this and the personal urgency which gives tension, then her poems lose their impact. Her least effective poems lapse into didacticism and social affirmation rather than personal affirmation."

THE LAND OF SILENCE AND OTHER POEMS, 1953

Bogan, Louise. "Verse," New Yorker. 30 (February 27, 1954), 101.

"In her fourth volume of verse Sarton begins to show signs of an insight 'into the life of things'." The collection is too long in parts, notes Bogan, and is conventionally literary, but at least a dozen poems exhibit Sarton's mature power of "... recognizing the heart of the matter and of expressing it in memorable terms."

Booklist and Subscription Books Bulletin. 50 (October 1, 1953), 51.

The reviewer describes the verse in this volume as "... sensitive and delicately haunting lyrical poems and sonnets. Sarton captures the evanescent moods of nature and transitory experiences of the human heart ... in love and in friendship."

Ciardi, John. "Recent Verse," Nation. 178 (February 27, 1954), 184.

"Sarton relies too heavily on 'high pitched' adjectives which have no specific sensory content. All of them assert, distinct from 'objectify,' an emotion in the past. The emotional assertion seems always to be made without regard for the object. Her poetry asserts pregenerated emotion--it is distinct from and inferior to the type of poetry that generates its emotion in its own movement."

Deutsch, Babette. "Poetry Chronicle," Yale Review. 43 (Winter, 1954), 280.

Deutsch recognizes Sarton's technical competency but believes something to be missing in her poetry. "There is a tendency to more statement than the poem requires, and a peculiar feminine quality in the sonnet sequences. Sometimes they lapse into the conventional and the tone is too personal." ... "The lack in these poems seems to be due to Sarton's inability to be severe with herself."

Fowlie, Wallace. "A Package of Poetry," New Republic. 129 (December 14, 1953), 19.

"In this volume Sarton demonstrates a great range of feeling and subject, an unusual strength in describing what comes before her eyes and touches her heart." ... "In 'Letter From Chicago' and especially in 'These Images Remain' her words have an unexpected newness. The ease with which images in her poetry transpose notions provides the ... abstractions with their own firmness and poetic vigor."

Kirkus Review. 21 (July 15, 1953), 473.

"Sensuous, sensitive and perceptive, the poems reveal a deeper dimension, touching on the metaphysical. Sarton's mastery of form is not quite equal to her intensity and purity of feeling." In essence, the reviewer believes that the poems in this volume do not live up to a "... marriage of form and content, but poetry lovers will thank Sarton for an enjoyable and uplifting hour."

Library Journal. 78 (December 15, 1953), 2221.

"These distinguished lyrics, sensitive yet forceful,

project the life of nature and the poetry of life. Journeys and recognitions recur, as well as themes of exile and the community."

Lucas, Alec. The Fiddlehead Quarterly. 19 (November, 1953), 13-15.

Sarton, in this volume, has universalized the personal. "Although she is individualistic, although she is frequently subtle and minute in examining her sensitivities, she is seldom obscure and can communicate her own vision to the reader directly and simply." Sarton's poetry lacks power, though, according to Lucas. "Sensitive and intelligent, rather than passionate and intellectual, Miss Sarton's verse is characterized by vivid imagery, simplicity and freshness of diction, and restraint."

McCormick, John. "Poet and Anti-Poet," Western Review. 19 (Autumn, 1954), 71-72.

"Although it is unchivalrous, I can only conclude that Sarton writes as though the 20th century has never happened. In her verses one finds a strange, latter-day pantheism, a wealth of damnable botanizing. They are personal verses that never become universal." ... "Technically, she is accomplished; her sonnet sequence is elegant, with wide variety of verse form. But, she writes in only one key, whatever the subject or the form."

Meyer, Gerard. "Conscious Art," Saturday Review of Literature. 37 (January 16, 1954), 19.

"Sarton ... is a mistress of the neatly turned concluding line, which may be described as both her strength and her weakness. Her skill and percipience sometimes just save her from banality." ..."It is perhaps her intellectualism (or ours!) that makes one over-conscious at times of her use of the quick, colloquial thrust, and the telling, sudden word that defines the moment and the scene."

Nemerov, Howard. "Contemporary Poets," Atlantic Monthly. 194 (September, 1954), 67.

A close reading of Sarton, according to Nemerov, is disappointing. "Most of the poems are marred by a false concept of poetry as a free excitement unattached to the hardness of things--a eleutheromania." ... "Either there is a flatness where excitement is intended or some violent feeling expressed for its own sake."

United States Quarterly Book Review. 10 (March, 1954), 55.
The reviewer notes that although Sarton's poems are perceptive in feeling and initial lines are intense and musical, she does not sustain this throughout. "The endings tend to become facile summaries or assertions. Some of the poems in this volume are good and show advancement over past achievements, especially the sonnet sequence 'These Images Remain'." "Sarton is an observant and candid woman."

IN TIME LIKE AIR, 1958

Derleth, August. Voices. 167 (September-December, 1958), 54-56.
Derleth writes, "... these are poems written from acute observation, reflective poems, the simplicity of which only conceals searching depths. Her verse is sensitive, her form exacting, and her subjects those which will appeal to literate readers...."

Dickey, James. "In the Presence of Anthologies," Sewanee Review. 66 (Spring, 1958), 306-307.
"May Sarton is not a profoundly original writer, but she is a beautiful one, with a casual balance, the womanly assurance and judiciousness not found in many other women poets. In almost every poem she attains a delicate simplicity, direct and deeply given. She is the queen of a small, well-ordered country."

Hazel, Robert. "Three New Volumes," Poetry. 94 (August, 1959), 343-346.
"Many of Sarton's lyrics suffer from neatness and surrender to homiletic bathos. Her work depends on regularity and the stylistic assurance that mastery of rhythmic predictability entails and on meticulous writing of moral and philosophical inklings that a consistent view provides. 'Reflection in a Double Mirror' and 'Death and the Lovers' are total coalescence of idiom and insight." As a minor fault, Hazel believes the volume should have been weeded, "... it would have been impeccable with half its contents."

Holden, Raymond. "Passion and Grief, Music," New York

Times Book Review, December 22, 1957, p. 5.
In Sarton's writing there is passion, discretion, grief, joy, music and the intimation of delight. Her work is distinguished by its simplicity. "... her extraordinary gift is the ability to make the actualities of physical existence and motion serve as the imaginative metaphor pointing to metaphysical reality."

Holmes, John. "Poets of Maturity and Art," New York Herald Tribune/Book Review, January 26, 1958, p. 4.
"Sarton writes with sharp wit in 'Dialogue' and calmed intensity in 'At Muzot'." "In this book the poet's intangibles, as subjects, become real, and her subjectives become impersonal enough to be shared. The title poem is a metaphor for love dissolving self, to crystalize as detachment."

Kirkus Review. 25 (September 1, 1957), 677.
"Sarton, with this volume of poetry, has overreached herself to a certain extent. Many of the poems lack the immediacy of her earlier work." But there are exceptions, the reviewer notes, and they are worth reading, especially "A Celebration" and some of the sonnets.

Library Journal. 83 (April 1, 1958), 1100.
"The growing body of poems by Sarton is matched by a growth in her own ability and in her own control over the varied themes to which she turns."

New Yorker. 34 (March 22, 1958), 156.
"Sarton does not subject her material to the crucial tensions usual in modern poetry, but it would be a mistake to place her at a remove from the moderns, since her wit and insight are sharply contemporary, while her subject matter is ... timeless." ... "She is contemplative and exploratory."

CLOUD, STONE, SUN, VINE: POEMS SELECTED AND NEW, 1961

Fuson, Ben. Library Journal. 87 (February 1, 1962), 565.
"Sarton's sure technique and effortless word-mastery coupled with pungent metaphysical insights make this volume an exquisite residuum of twenty years of assiduous craftsmanship and inner vision."

Morse, Samuel. "A Baker's Dozen," Virginia Quarterly Review. 38 (Spring, 1962), 328.

According to Morse, Sarton's most moving poems are those that can be properly described as "domestic." "The political poems drift into a kind of abstract eloquence that is unpersuasive." He sees the new poems as the most rewarding.

Shapiro, Karl. "Voices That Speak to the Critic in Very Different Rhythms." New York Times Book Review, December 24, 1961, p. 4.

"Sarton is a bad poet. Her poetry is lady-poetry at its worst. Her high literary attitudes (Rilke and Yeats) are only hastily mastered techniques gaily applied for the occasion." "Her poems are a chamber of cliches." Shapiro ends by saying, "... it is pointless to be cruel about bad poetry, ... sometimes there is no escape...."

Webster, Harvey Curtis. "Five Poets," Poetry. 101 (December, 1962), 211-212.

"As one would expect of a book 144 pages long there are poems bad enough to justify Karl Shapiro's recent exclamation against Sarton. Nevertheless, I think she is a fine poet much of the time. Sometimes there is too easy facility in management of metrics and too little severity in her choice of words but often times she redeems herself." "'These Images Remain' are unobtrusively expert sonnets."

A PRIVATE MYTHOLOGY, 1966

Bennet, Joseph. "Indian, Greek and Japanese," New York Times Book Review, November 13, 1966, p. 6.

"Sarton's poems about India are remarkable for their savage brilliance. She was offended by India, and unprepared; her response has the power of resentment and struggle." "The poems about Japan and Greece are not as good; they have the quality of notes thought out in advance."

Booklist and Subscription Books Bulletin. 62 (June 15, 1966), 968.

A very brief review in which the reviewer remarks that the poems of Japan are noted as reflecting in form the austerity and colorfulness of an ancient civilization.

Clements, Robert J. "The Muses Are Herd," Saturday Review. 49 (May 21, 1966), 31.

"Miss Sarton's power to recall and evocation of nostalgia are considerable."

Curley, Dorothy. Library Journal. 91 (February 1, 1966), 700.

Curley writes of the poems in this volume as "... modest but not particularly interesting verse." "Sarton's superficial knowledge of the countries visited hinders her ability to accurately describe them." ... "Sarton is unwilling to tell much about herself." Finally, Curley views it as a "... mildly pleasant, slightly inspirational volume for women."

Freeman, Arthur. "Five Poets," Poetry. 109 (December, 1966), 192-193.

"Sarton's free verse permits a suppleness, a fluidity and a language stripped of elaboration, but the results seem frequently a little lax. Some of the Japanese poems are slack, falsely epigrammatic 'solutions' in which the insignificant is stressed and left over delicacy, deference, and politeness."

Kirkus Review. 34 (January 15, 1966), 89.

"The poems dealing with Greece, Japan and India are tourist snapshots which externalize some of the bewilderment and displacement abroad." ... "The second section of poems displays great assurance as well as contrast both in approach and time."

McMichael, James. "Pound and Others," Southern Review. 3 (Spring, 1967), 435-436.

"Many of the poems in this volume are occasional in nature, and many are devoted almost exclusively to sensory impressions. The process of Sarton's learning is too self-conscious and the products are dull too much of the time. Her free verse is handled more successfully than the traditional line in which many of the poems are consistently bad, filled with clumsy iambs."

Morse, Samuel. "Poetry," Wisconsin Studies in Contemporary Literature. 9 (Winter, 1968), 112.

This criticism consists of six brief lines: the critic praises Sarton for writing "... delicate, precise images with surprisingly pointed and personal insights."

... "Sarton continues to provide the reader with works of 'standard' quality."

Pritchard, William. "Poetry Chronicle," Hudson Review. 20 (Summer, 1967), 306.

The critic sees Sarton's writing as condescending and overblown. "She is also patronizing in her remarks about Japan." ... "... her poetry is too trite and deals with stylized subjects."

Ruffin Carolyn. "From the Book Review Shelf: A Voice of Tender Protest," Christian Science Monitor, June 10, 1967, p. 9.

Ruffin writes that the poems in this volume are not epic but they do create a private mythology. She sees a relationship between the poems in the first section and those in the second in that "... the places visited, with their mysteries and contrasts, become meaningful in the context of her (Sarton's) own surroundings."

Stephens, Alan. "Twelve New Books of Poetry, 1966," Denver Quarterly. 1 (Winter, 1967), 101-112.

"Sarton is intelligent and likeable--you can trust her to not pull any dismaying stunts. Her work isn't of the first intensity but the poems make pleasant reading."

Urdang, Constance. "Gregor, Sarton, Vazakas," Poetry. 112 (April, 1968), 44.

"Sarton is a 'non-poet's poet'; she possesses cultivation, humility, fluidity and is civilized and accomplished, and for this reason, out of style for today." ... "The virtues Sarton's verse possess are still valued in real life by educated middle class people, but no longer have value in literature."

Vendler, Helen. "Recent American Poetry," Massachusetts Review. 8 (Summer, 1967), 557.

"May Sarton is a derivative poet, and she lives in a rarefied and self-regarding aloofness. There is no surprise in her poetry; it deals in almost all the cliches of literate verse."

Wilson, Robley. Carleton Miscellany. 8 (Winter, 1967), 106.

In this six line review Wilson notes that Sarton writes poetry in short free lines, "... the sort one could read all day without falling asleep or catching the breath."

AS DOES NEW HAMPSHIRE, 1967

Booklist and Subscription Books Bulletin. 64 (January 15, 1968), 579.

A brief, five line review in which Sarton's poems are described as "well crafted verse."

A GRAIN OF MUSTARD SEED, 1971

Marvin, Patricia. Library Journal. 96 (March 1, 1971), 839.

Marvin views the subject matter of the poems as contemporary (strife, madness of lost values, etc.) but the tone as one of a mature, gentle sadness. "... there is a profound simplicity which often masks complexity." "Sarton sensitively observes nature and man evolving through growth in time."

Reeve, F. D. "In My Father's House," Poetry. 121 (March, 1973), 348-355.

Reeve, in this review of nine books of poetry, places the poets in a "play"; each poet/author taking part and speaking lines from their own poems. The general tone of the "play" is one of disgust on the part of Reeve. The poets, when confronted with a critic, kick and abuse him and turn to the reader (audience) as the only one who can give meaning to their works.

Taylor, Henry. "A Gathering of Poets," Western Humanities Review. 25 (Autumn, 1971), 4.

"A merging of political and other human realities in a sensibility that may previously have separated them creates interesting tensions in this volume. Too few of the public poems arise from the powers of sympathy associated with Sarton's mature poems. They strain against self-consciousness. She is still fighting the isolation which has helped her find her best poems so far; when she comes to terms with the right balance of isolation and involvement, she will have mastered what seems tentative here."

________. Masterplots 1972 Annual. Ed. Frank N. Magill.

Englewood Cliffs, New Jersey: Salem Press, 1972, pp. 155-158.

The publication of A Private Mythology marked a new direction for Sarton and suggested that her earlier poetry had offered more than some readers had perceived. Her poems began to explore nature in contrast with the uglier aspects of life, as well as revealing an increasing knowledge of mortality. A Grain of Mustard Seed displays this continuing concern with these problems and broadens the scope of Sarton's subject matter. Taylor sees a minor fault in Sarton's self-consciousness in dealing with political themes but this failure does not detract from the strength of the poems as a whole.

A DURABLE FIRE, 1972

Brown, Rosellen. "Plenitude and Dearth," Parnassus: Poetry in Review. 1 (Spring/Summer, 1973), 49-50.

"There are many brief evocations of an actual rural world, but it is, every bit of it, so used and directed, that what is concrete in it melts and refreezes as yet another impenetrable abstraction. So while this kind of poetry appears superficially to work by equivalencies of fact with emotions, nothing in the end has its own real life to begin from: it is all props on which, we are assured, great inner consequences lean." Brown does admit that "... here and there one can find lovely single lines." "The Fear of Angels" Brown notes was one of the more convincing poems in the volume.

Choice. 9 (November, 1972), 1132.

In these poems "... the reader is caught up into a life current that startles him into a new awareness of the human dynamo and its capacity for joy and misery." The reviewer points to the moments of deep stillness and quiet wisdom as well as passionate explosions in many of the poems. "Sarton's voice has achieved amazing strength and vigor."

O'Hara, T. Best Sellers. 32 (May 1, 1972), 69.

"These poems lack vigor; they lack drama for echoes, and succeed, when they do, without benefit of energetic language. There is a tendency toward 'limp speech'." ... "Although her subjects are reminiscent of Frost and Thoreau, Sarton has neither the range nor the power of these writers."

Smith, Ray. Permanent Fires: Reviews of Poetry, 1958-1973. Metuchen, New Jersey: Scarecrow Press, 1975, pp. 95-96.

"As poetry, carefully wrought, its conspicuous values are clarity and precision in the perceptions of country things and of emotions felt in solitude. The poetry loses its balance and weaves in and out of triteness through inordinate pursuit and repetition of a pre-ordained theme."

COLLECTED POEMS, 1930-1973, 1974

Chasin, Helen. "May Sarton," Village Voice, June 13, 1974, pp. 36-38.

This review concerns itself mainly with Sarton's novel, Mrs. Stevens Hears the Mermaids Singing, but there is a reference to Collected Poems, with a short comment about the "intellectual poems."

Choice. 11 (October, 1974), 1140.

"This volume contains the major themes that Sarton has become known for, all culminating in a self-awareness and self-knowledge on the part of the poet. The chronological order of the poems reveals Sarton's progression of manipulation and artistry."

Etter, Dave. "Current Collections," American Libraries. 5 (November, 1974), 548.

In an overall review of current anthologies of poetry, Etter refers to Sarton's Collected Poems as highly readable and satisfying.

Harris, James Neil. Green River Review. 6 (Summer, 1975), 103-105.

"Sarton's Collected Poems is a volume well worth the reader's collection and the poet's recollection." Harris notes that Sarton is first concerned with form; the poem is treated as an aesthetic and organized whole. This form is specifically the "classic form"; the Shakespearean sonnet sequence, villanelle, haiku, etc. Sarton is also concerned with the state of the world, with the need for love, the responsibility of the artist, moral order and artistic order, role of men and the potentiality of women, self-revelation and self-control.

"The creative impulse and the making of poetry are her expression of affirmation." The volume as a whole traces the maturation of Sarton's verse.

Knies, Elizabeth. Commonweal. 102 (July 4, 1975), 252.
"What is striking in Collected Poems is the craftsmanship, control and inspiration that permeate Sarton's work. The poetry records many tangible things, but primarily it is a testimony to an enduring inwardness." "May Sarton has been celebrated as a great solitary; like Colette's, her prose writings on the subject ... provide insights into the life of one who has lived alone. The poetry amplified this theme a hundred-fold, examining ... the process of time and change." Knies finally remarks, "... this body of work intelligently conceived and finely wrought, is the consummation of a distinguished career and a major achievement in its own right."

Martin, James. "Questions of Style," Poetry. 15 (May, 1975), 114-115.
In his review of eight new volumes of poetry, Martin writes of May Sarton's Collected Poems, "May Sarton's poems enter and illuminate every natural corner of our lives." In her forty plus years of writing, she has made a "... pertinent, enduring testament." Martin notes that Sarton has the ability to harness a "good violence" in an "organic form." "May Sarton's poems are so strong in their faith and in their positive response to the human condition that they will likely outlast much of the fashionable, cynical poetry of our era."

Taylor, Henry. "Home to a Place Beyond Exile: The Collected Poems of May Sarton," The Hollins Critic. 11 (June, 1974), 1-16.
Taylor reviews the poetry in Collected Poems as an overall view of Sarton's writing career and life. "Sarton designed (the volume) with the lifelong process in view; she wished to reveal the development of her career and of a person." Her themes include the feminine condition, art, love, landscape, travel, search for a lasting home and exploration of an inner violence. Overall, there is a didactic tone which makes her unique; didactism with a positive quality and within the historical bounds of poetry. Taylor examines key poems from Sarton's previous volumes, noting their part

in the "rounding-out" of her creativity. By examining her poetry as a whole, Taylor contends, one can perceive the cycles through which she has evolved.

Thomas, William V. "Two Books from an Author Whose Audience May at Last Be Ready for Her," Washington, D.C. Star-News, September 1, 1974, n.p.

In his review of Collected Poems, Thomas writes, "Sarton makes sense out of suffering and loss by removing the experience to a realm where it can at least be understood if not fully controlled ..." ... "Experience is painful, and Sarton's poems explore the various agencies of naturalistic shock." Thomas sees Sarton's best poems as those in which they "... dwell on the subject of form, the artist's range to impose order on the unruly flux of experience...."

BOOK REVIEWS / NOVELS

THE SINGLE HOUND, 1938

Benet, William. "Poet Divided," Saturday Review of Literature. 18 (June 11, 1938), 13.

Benet views this work as a novel of exceptional quality. "Her prose strikes one as more mature and finished than her poetry. Her prose is a beautiful skill throughout."

Beresford, J. D. "Novels by Women," Manchester Guardian, April 29, 1938, p. 7.

"The Single Hound is by way of being a museum piece, carefully polished and no less carefully displayed to exhibit the gracefulness of its lines." According to Beresford, the novel is a graceful, well-considered book, with "... only just the hint of an American accent."

Feld, Rose. "The Heart of the Poet, in Youth and in Age," New York Herald Tribune/Books, March 20, 1938, p. 5.

"One is enmeshed in beauty of words which reach into the inner chambers of human fears and confusions." The story will be remembered, writes Feld, and the book reread for the beauty of characterization. "Sarton's work will speak in a familiar tongue to all human beings."

Hartley, L. P. "The Literary Lounger," The Sketch (London), May 11, 1938, p. 312.

"In this novel Sarton has brought together two worlds, the world of sense and the world of spirit, and reconciled them. The deepest reality of the novel is centered in the scenes in Ghent. If Mark had not gone there and come to his understanding with Doro, this reality may never have come into focus." Hartley criticizes the novel only because of Sarton's tendency to lapse into idiom, but overall, views it as a work of art.

Mann, Dorothea. Boston Transcript, April 9, 1938, p. 2.
"In some ways it is a very mature book and in others a young book reflecting as only a young author can the moods and thoughts of her generation." "The dramatic quality of the dynamic force of Mark and Doro add to the understanding and beauty found in the novel."

"New First Novels," Time Literary Supplement (London), April 30, 1938, p. 298.
"Sarton's first novel is a generous and pleasant book." ... "The book, unusual in theme and atmosphere, will impress Sarton's name on the discerning reader."

New Republic. 94 (April 6, 1938), 286.
The critic views the novel as written in a "... delicate manner," with "... tones so hushed and subtle that some of the implications do not filter through."

Powell, Dilys. "A Modern Cranford," Sunday Times (London), April 24, 1938, p. 10.
"Sarton's first novel deals with intangibles yet the scene of this uneventful, almost static story is pencilled in with unrelaxed fidelity...." The first part of the book is told with delicacy and hardly a touch of sentimentality. It is when the "world of action impinges on the world of withdrawal from action that Sarton is less sure of herself."

Reid, Forrest. "Fiction," Spectator. 160 (April 29, 1938), 770.
Reid recognizes this as a carefully written novel but not impressive. The characters are too "... whimsical and clever to be taken seriously."

Shawe-Taylor, Desmond. "New Novels," New Statesman and Nation, May 7, 1938, p. 795.
"Sarton allows her style to 'sag' at times in this novel. The little old ladies are self-conscious--the nature of the 'illumination' which Doro, the older poet, transmits to Mark is not clear." Yet, part of the book is the affair between Mark and the painter, "... a quiet little rivulet ... almost submerged by a

continuous spate of thought-stream on both sides but with moments of real insight none the less."

Southron, Jane. "The Single Hound and Other Works of Fiction," New York Times Book Review, March 20, 1938, p. 6.

This novel is described by Southron as a beautiful and distinguished first publication. "It is a stark, plain tale with a rush of fire in it. There is not a sense of poetry gone astray into prose." ... "In this novel Sarton has exemplified a way of life and enunciated a literary creed. It is not autobiographical but personal."

Swinnerton, Frank. "Ordeals and Endings," The Observer (London), April 24, 1938, p. 6.

"Individualism, simplicity, purity of heart, this novel returns to these fundamentals." Because the story, and the age is illuminated, the critic praises it, but faults what he calls a "precocity of approach." "... the vignettes of the London aesthetic scenes show glimpses of a talent with a future."

Time. 31 (March 21, 1938), 79.

The novel is described as a "... plaintive first novel by a twenty-six year old poetess, in which an aging spinster brings peace to a tormented young Englishman who is emotionally ravaged by an affair with a married woman."

Wisconsin Library Bulletin. 34 (July, 1938), 148.

"A story of unusual appeal for the discriminating, of the friendship that develops between two poets, one an elderly Belgian woman, one a lonely young Englishman who has found comfort in her poems, not knowing her identity."

THE BRIDGE OF YEARS: 1946

Bond, Alice Dixon. "The Case for Books," The Boston Herald, May 8, 1946, p. 38.

With the publication of The Bridge of Years, Bond believes that Sarton has achieved genuine distinction as a novelist. "It is a book of high purpose and rich understanding, full-textured and emotionally sound." "This is a tender, gently rendered novel which is warmly human and very satisfying."

Bookmark. 7 (November, 1946), 15.
The reviewer describes the novel as "... a delicate, perceptive chronicle." "Melanie, the energetic business woman, warm-hearted and lovable, journeys, with her family, over the 'bridge of years' which leads to a second world catastrophe in the form of World War II."

Bullock, Florence Haxton. "Pilgrim's Progress of a Family: 1919-1940," New York Herald Tribune/Weekly Book Review, April 21, 1946, p. 5.
This novel shows how one intelligent, moral European family built up its strength to endure and resist the Nazi surge. Sarton's style is "... unpretentious, beautifully expressive, and warmly and humanly emotional."

D. B. B. "Between the Wars: The Bridge of Years, Story of a Belgian Family," Springfield Republican, June 9, 1946, p. 4d.
This story is essentially about Melanie Duchesne, whose indomitable spirit keeps her family together during the trying Nazi occupation of Belgium. "Miss Sarton knows her ground thoroughly, and her people. You come to know them too, not only what they say and do but what they think and feel."

Frank, Grace. "Belgium Between Wars," Saturday Review of Literature. 29 (October 26, 1946), 33.
Describing the novel as a "... beautifully wrought book, deeply felt, ..." Frank writes, "Sarton understands the lonely inviolability of the individual and the universal need for love without bondage. She also understands the eternal dilemma of those torn between the life of the spirit and life as it must be lived on a more human plane."

Maher, Catherine. "Self-Searching Between Wars," New York Times Book Review, April 21, 1946, p. 26.
Maher believes Sarton's novel, if not brilliant, is always interesting, competently written and distinguished by its honesty and its broad plan of inquiry.

New Yorker. 22 (April 27, 1946), 89.
A brief review in which the novel is described as

a delicately done chronicle. "Not everybody's dish, but one which exudes a special, if at times faint, flavor."

Soskind, William. "Books and Things," New York Herald Tribune, April 27, 1946, p. 10.

Soskind notes that Sarton appreciates the basic realities of a home, its confusion, crises and constant turmoil, and of a marriage relationship. "All this she describes lyrically and with great feeling so that she carries her reader with her in the flight from a politically cursed, socially barren world. She has drawn the magic circle of home around a group of ... people, and rescued them from the ... insecurity which surrounds most of us. That is the chief appeal of her novel."

SHADOW OF A MAN, 1950

Booklist and Subscription Books Bulletin. 46 (May 1, 1950), 2761.

The novel is briefly described as a "... subtly told story of emotional growing pains, perhaps too finely spun for some readers."

Bookmark. 9 (July, 1950), 244.

In a one line statement the reviewer acknowledges that this novel is beautifully written, yet "... sophisticated; for the mature reader."

"Briefly Noted Fiction," New Yorker. 26 (May 6, 1950), 114.

The critic argues that the affair between Francis and his French lover is dropped too suddenly and much too easily by Sarton, "... whose smooth, intelligent writing is somewhat spoiled by her impatience, or reluctance, when it comes to dealing with a 'climax'."

Butcher, Fanny. "Genius Seen in a Novel by May Sarton," Chicago Sunday Tribune, May 7, 1950, p. 4.

"Poetic genius vibrates through every line of this book. Sarton's novel has qualities, tones and overtones seldom met in present day popular writing. Her translation of a character's reaction to places is as memorable as her recording of the inter-reactions of their human contacts."

"Characters in a Play," Times Literary Supplement (London), April 11, 1952, p. 249.

Francis Chabrier, the protagonist in this novel, ... "is never convincing, nor, alas, very interesting; and below its thin gloss of sophistication, Shadow of a Man is a sentimental little tale."

Christian Science Monitor. June 10, 1950, p. 8.

The character development in this novel, according to the critic, seems oversimplified and melodramatic, but plausible within the limits. Sarton's description of France is more believable for she brings warmth and atmosphere to the scenes. "... her writing is a delight."

Douglas, Marjory Stoneman. "Devil in the Flesh," Saturday Review of Literature. 33 (August 12, 1950), 10.

Douglas compares Sarton's novel to Henry James' The Ambassadors, with the conclusion that Sarton's talent is "... such that her work does not suffer by comparison." The critic asks how much value Francis' teaching will have in the small mid-western school with an aura that comes from being an heir of the rich tradition of French and Bostonian culture. "How well can a man teach who under such a cloak hides the slow withering-before-ripeness or the fatty degeneration of emotional impurity of a will that is never exercised?" Unlike James' protagonist, "Francis has not progressed toward the end of all conscious living."

Dunlap, Katherine. "Boston to France: A Young Man in Revolt," The Philadelphia Inquirer Magazine, June 4, 1950, p. 39.

"May Sarton is a gifted novelist and poet, and the high level of her writing is maintained throughout the story, which is peopled with articulate thinking men and women." "... there are fine lines written with the poet's touch as the author is inspired by the mystic qualities of thought in the Cathedral of Chartres."

Garrigue, Jean. "Brief Comment," New Republic. 122 (May 8, 1950), 20.

The critic describes the novel as one of sensibility oversimplified. "Being a novel of sensibility without, actually, a real situation, its wisdom and cultivation of spirit do not come to grips with any of the problems suggested by the education of the hero." "... the story of a young man found who has been lost is told too glibly. At worst, it is woman's magazine writing; at best, it treats of serious matters too easily."

Kirkus Review. 18 (March 1, 1950), 144.
"A very simple story, rather obliquely and beautifully told, of a young man, at war with himself." ... "A mature love story with idyllic overtones and a satisfying ending for romanticists."

Laycock, Edward A. "Education of a Bostonian," The Boston Sunday Globe, May 14, 1950, p. A59.
According to Laycock, Sarton deals expertly with Boston and Bostonians. "Bostonians should enjoy her novel because of the homely familiar things in it, because of its intellectual quality and its clarity." ... "Her prose is a delight to read."

Newsweek. 35 (May 8, 1950), 95.
"This is a sensitive and well rounded fictional portrait...." ..."It is a novel of unexpected depths and transparent prose."

Sardrock, Mary. Catholic World. 171 (August, 1950), 394.
"It is difficult to share Sarton's intense concern for the plight of Francis ... he suffers from a specialized form of momism." The critic commends Sarton's prose for its delicate and charming expression, but overall, the novel is weakened by "... flabby characterization and illogical motivation."

Snow, C. P. "To Dream Again," Sunday Times (London), April 20, 1952, p. 3.
The novel is an "... urbane study of the outer edges of sensibility, evocative, romantic and not as profound as a first impression may suggest." "... it is hard to believe in the rude young man with the tender heart, and harder still to accept the worldly, tragic charmer as anything more than a type made familiar by fiction."

Snyder, Marjory. "Shadow of a Man Fascinating Novel," New York Herald Tribune, May 28, 1950, p. 6.
"When a poet becomes a novelist the result is beautiful rhythmic prose, a delicate choice of theme, an honesty and clarity in character creation."

Taylor, Helen. Library Journal. 75 (May 1, 1950), 775.
According to Taylor this novel affords a "... minimum of action and plot but sensitive writing."

Walton, Edith. "Four Titles from the Field of Current Fiction," New York Times Book Review, May 11, 1950, p. 20.
Sarton's book is full of lyric charm. It is sensitive, perceptive, alive to delicate shades of feeling. But, Walton notes, Sarton takes Francis too "portentously"; he is not as attractive and interesting to the reader as to the creator. "One does not believe that Francis' difficulties can be solved so easily." "... as a whole, it is a provocative and appealing novel."

Young, Viola. "Its Theme: 'To Thine Own Self Be True'," New York Herald Tribune/Book Review, May 28, 1950, p. 6.
Young believes this to be a finely written and sensitive novel that opens with "death out of which there comes life." "It is a quiet, restrained and dignified book, warm and compelling; it deserves to be read for itself."

A SHOWER OF SUMMER DAYS, 1952

Ames, Alfred. "Lovers and Loved in Irish Summer Novel of High and Quiet Quality," Chicago Sunday Tribune, November 30, 1952, p. 4.
Ames writes, "... the novel is a serious interpretation of life, executed with artistry. The events are feelings, not action." "Rising action is one of growing discipline, and the outcome is achievement for freedom." ... "Although the novel is limited in scope, it is not limited in quality."

Booklist and Subscription Books Bulletin. 49 (November 1, 1952), 90.
The reviewer regards this novel as a gently probing story of the interrelationship of four people and the effect on them of the remote Irish country house where they are brought together. "Fine writing but the appeal may be limited to the discriminating."

Bookmark. 12 (December, 1952), 56.
This novel, notes the critic, is for the discriminating reader. Violet is described as "middle-aged,"

Charles as "attractive but philandering," and the niece as "intense." Their relationship evolves in the subtle atmosphere of Dene's Court.

"Briefly Noted Fiction," New Yorker. 28 (October 25, 1952), 152-153.
An intricate, planned story in which the "... ending is unsatisfactory because it doesn't seem very true, but the writing is thoughtful and direct, the people are all alive and conscious of each other, and the house is wonderful."

Carr, Susan. "Boston Author's Newest Novel Shows Insight into Character," Wellesley College News, December 4, 1952, p. 2.
"In the same manner that it is rare to find a combination of poetry and realism in a novel, it is also unusual to read a novel in which complex ... characters are able to resolve their problems successfully." "The Novel combines the qualities of prose and poetry in a meaningful and sensitive fashion, and leaves one with a ... feeling of having communicated with a house, its inhabitants, and a poetess."

"Domestic Circles," Times Literary Supplement (London), September 19, 1954, p. 569.
"Miss Sarton is clever and quick and shrewd enough to make her mark with people in conflict, but here her theme is wasted by a woefully inadequate treatment."

Feld, Rose. "Shimmering and Melodic," New York Herald Tribune/Book Review, October 26, 1952, p. 6.
According to Feld this novel has the quality of "... a musical tone poem, with a touch delicate and penetrating, in which Sarton explores the character of Violet in relation to the other characters and the house." "In the final pages she brings her theme into full orchestration." "... here it is that the continually stirring portrait of Violet receives the final strokes that raise it to magnificence."

Gannett, Lewis. "Books and Things," New York Herald Tribune, October 31, 1952, p. 27.
"... there is intense distilled living in May Sarton's nov about four people whose lives it [Dene's Court] changed." Gannett believes that Sarton has a subtle understanding of the meaning of love, loyalty and innocence and is able

to "skillfully combine these in this novel." "Miss Sarton's perceptions have something of the exquisite tenuousness of a whiff from a flower garden. Her book will never top the best-seller list, but it will give an almost aching delight to a limited, perhaps feminine, circle of readers."

Hay, Sara Henderson. "Husband's Burden," Saturday Review. 35 (November 29, 1952), 18.

"The intricate pattern of emotional relationships in Dene's Court is almost too large for the novel. So much has to be settled that at times actions and reactions are explained rather than allowed, by implication and suggestion, to make their own significant revelation." Hay believes that Sally's personality is so complex that some of the 'right about faces' she makes seem insufficiently dealt with. But, the character of Violet is complete and well drawn. As a whole, the novel is "rewarding and memorable."

Kirkus Review. 20 (August 15, 1952), 519.

The reviewer briefly states that in the novel there are "... private worlds of tranquility and unrest, of fugitive perception and fitful intensity, suggestively transcribed for the audience of Elizabeth Bowen."

Lewis, R. W. B. "Eccentrics' Pilgrimage," Hudson Review. 6 (Spring, 1953), 144-146.

"In a pleasant way this novel is old-fashioned. The small graceful and somewhat untidy world of Dene's Court might have fallen apart if tempers had been shorter, if lusts had been less controlled by habits of humor and wisdom, or if Sarton had been less bold. At the end Sally finds herself 'inside' but not trapped, alone and free." Lewis sees the denouement as a Jamesian anecdote, relationships never stay put, but are constantly dissolving, reforming and shifting. "Her writing is not as fluid as James' but the controlling vision is, and evenly diffused. Miss Sarton's lyrical and sensuous narrative always seems to know its own strength, which while modest is irreducible."

Nerber, John. "The Shabby Great," New York Times Book Review, October 26, 1952, p. 4.

Nerber ranks this novel with the very best of her distinguished novels and establishes once and for all "... Sarton's unmistakable authority. Violet is never reduced to the novelist's mercy--she is so complete. It is a first rate literary creation."

"Not Getting On," Times Literary Supplement (London), April 4, 1953, p. 181.

"Miss Sarton can compete with Virginia Woolf in her unhurried analysis of a woman's private emotional world, but she gives rather too clinical an impression in her conclusions--conclusions which, because they are drawn by the characters themselves, exude a smugness Mrs. Woolf always escaped."

Raleigh, John Henry. "Four New Novels," New Republic. 127 (December 8, 1952), 28.

According to Raleigh the subject matter of the novel is "... civilized, upper-class Anglo-Irish, reminiscent of Henry James, its tone and attitude, a pervasive and persuasive feminism, suggests Virginia Woolf." "Sally has her final 'epiphany' by mastering feelings; she had come to understand the meaning of discipline and its reward: freedom and power." Sarton has handled the traditional form and subject matter exceptionally well. "She never fails to see complexity and never gives in to sentimentality."

Rugg, Winnifred. "Assorted New Novels," Christian Science Monitor, December 24, 1952, p. 11.

"Shower of Summer Days is an Elizabeth Bowen kind of book, delicate, complex perceptions conveyed in a tone of lightest irony. The house is not merely a setting but a chief character. The story, like the house, has a certain discipline beneath its surface."

S. M. N. Springfield Republican, December 7, 1952, p. 7c.

In this short review the critic describes "Mary" (sic.) Sarton's novel as pleasant. "Dene's Court comes alive when Sally comes to live with her aunt and uncle."

Smith, Stevie. "New Novels," Observer (London), August 22, 1954, p. 7.

"It is a beautifully written, gentle story of honourable human beings' shifting affection." ... "Miss Sarton is as truthful as she is imaginative, though sometimes thin."

Tubby, Ruth. Library Journal. 77 (October 1, 1952), 1657.

"The plot is tenuous, most of the characters are

aimless and the appeal is largely derived from descriptions of flowers and the countryside. The whole is brilliant with unfulfilled possibilities as to a motivating purpose and plot development...."

Watts, Elizabeth. Boston Sunday Globe, October 26, 1952, p. A9.
Watts sees this book as a "delicate, powerful and thoroughly satisfying story of a woman who is trying to get her life in perspective." "Beyond the delicacy and delight there is a steady humor, too. This is a remarkable book."

Weeks, Edward. "The Peripatetic Reviewer," Atlantic Monthly. 191 (January, 1953), 80.
Weeks praises Sarton's sensitive affiliation with Europe. "Miss Sarton is at her poetic best in describing the moods of the house in sunlight and in rain...." The women are depicted better than the men, notes Weeks, but he appreciates Sarton's delineation of temperament and the "... skill with which she lets her men and women reveal themselves as they strive in cross-purpose and in intimacy to be true."

FAITHFUL ARE THE WOUNDS, 1955

Blotner, Joseph. The Modern American Political Novel, 1900-1960. Austin: University of Texas Press, 1966, pp. 322, 324.
Blotner discusses this novel as a bridge between the novel of disillusionment and that of the intellectual in politics. Cavan's convictions are only felt and appreciated after his death. "Sarton's style is effete and imitative but it is counterbalanced by a detailed portrayal of an intellectual."

Booklist and Subscription Books Bulletin. 51 (April, 1955), 317.
"Sarton ... drives home the issues which bedevil the modern intellectual in this novel." The reviewer offers a brief description of the novel's plot with little critical comment.

Bookmark. 14 (April, 1955), 162.
Briefly the reviewer comments that the story of

Cavan is described with impressive clarity in a striking portrait of a "champion of responsible citizenship."

"Briefly Noted Fiction," New Yorker. 31 (March 19, 1955), 150.

"The author's great and special talent is her ability to make her characters inexorably interlocked with each other the minute she starts writing about them." The critic views the epilogue as a terrible letdown to a good novel.

Connolly, Brendan. America. 93 (April 9, 1955), 48.

"Structurally, this novel simply fails to resolve the several problems, personal and social, which it raises. As an acute presentation of a frequent and perplexing psychological state, however, it is effective."

Crampton, Michael. "New Novels," New Statesman and Nation. 50 (November 19, 1955), 682.

Crampton notes that Sarton analyzes a universal malaise when she probes the attack on liberalism in America, but, unfortunately, at the end of the novel she makes no assessment: "... her exploratory torch shafts illuminatingly through the web of disintegrating Liberalism in America and plays fascinatingly about on Bostonian and Harvardian intellectual society."

Fiedler, Leslie A. "The War against the Academy," Wisconsin Studies in Contemporary Literature. 5 (Winter/Spring, 1964), 11.

In a reference to the factual death of F. O. Matthiessen, Fiedler briefly refers to Sarton's novel as a "successful attempt of academic tragedies."

Getlein, Frank, "Love and Violence: A Parable of Our Times," Commonweal. 62 (April 8, 1955), 19.

Getlein sees the novel as a "kaleidoscope of feeling." There is a maturity in Sarton's command of language, situation and character. "Although Cavan, the protagonist, emerges well, the reader is never brought inside him; he is revealed through the other characters' perspectives." Getlein reads the novel as basically a political work, "... Sarton catches the likeness of McCarthy better than most political attempts."

Goyen, William. "A Craving for Light," New York Times, March 13, 1955, p. 6.

Sarton's novel is "... a great and ever-deepening penetration into the darkness of uncommitted passion. Devoid of heroic exaggeration, the novel exists as a living segment of human life, serene and calmed, lonely, like its hero, in the face of shoddy fiction."

Havighurst, Walter. "Legacy of the Living," Saturday Review. 38 (March 19, 1955), 15.

The structure of the novel has a beautifully controlled tension; there is no anticlimax in the second half of the story. "Sarton has written a political novel for the 50's but it is more than political, it reveals a complex man in his total involvement--as a scholar, a teacher, a citizen." "It shows his tragic struggle to achieve communion with others and with himself, to live a whole life."

Hicks, Granville. "For Political Novels by Joseph Wechberg, Ralph de Toledano and May Sarton," The New Leader. 38 (March 28, 1955), 23-24.

"Miss Sarton has surrounded her Edward Cavan with a group of intensely interesting and admirably realized characters, and as she examines their relations with her protagonist, she explores some of the deepest problems of identity, friendship and love...." "To the sensibilities of a poet she adds sharp powers of observation and a fine sense of structure. Thus her book belongs to the small group of novels that transcend the public events with which they deal."

Kirkus Review. 23 (January 1, 1955), 18.

"This novel has none of the graceful, romantic properties of A Shower of Summer Days, but it's a thoughtful rather than forceful perspective of individuals and issues."

Lyons, John O. The College Novel in America. Illinois: Southern Illinois University Press, 1962, pp. 174-177, 179.

In his chapter "The Novel on Academic Freedom" Lyons views Sarton's novel as an "... impressive attempt to treat the question of academic freedom and the dilemma of the political liberal in the college." He sees this as a roman à clef due to the similarity between Edward Cavan and the real F. O. Matthiessen of Harvard who committed suicide in 1950. In this novel the reader is not distracted from the literature by the author's manipulation of the subject's real life. Sarton is faithful to the widely known facts of Matthiessen's life and death. "The excellent texture of the novel keeps it from becoming a gossip sheet."

Mitgong, Herbert. "Books of the Times," New York Times Book Review, March 26, 1955, p. 6.
"Being a skillful novelist and poet, Sarton probes the background and mind of Cavan. In the development of the story she depicts accurate scenes of Harvard and the teaching life." Unfortunately, Cavan remains "... a confused figure to the reader, there is not a complete fusion of the protagonist with the novel's retracing, but it does come close."

Peterson, Virgilia. "A Provocative Thesis Novel on a Great Teacher's Death," New York Herald Tribune/Book Review, March 13, 1955, p. 3.
Peterson describes Sarton as a moving and fastidious writer. Calling the novel a pièce à thèse, the critic sees it as "... a blow struck for the freedom of the mind ... that is in jeopardy." "Sometimes the ideas in the story overshadow and dominate the protagonist, but Sarton, enough of an artist and storyteller, is able to enlist her reader's sympathies."

Pickrel, Paul. "Outstanding Fiction: Some Political Novels," Yale Review. 44 (Summer, 1955), 637.
"On literary grounds, the book is open to reservations. One never really knows why Cavan commits suicide--Sarton hedges enough to show that she is ready to consider other explanations besides political but does not commit herself." The best thing about the novel, as Pickrel sees it, is its evocation of Boston and Cambridge. On the negative side, "... the book badly needs the depth of satire. Everything is taken very seriously, and with the same degree of seriousness."

Shrapnel, Norman. "New Novels," Manchester Guardian, November 8, 1955, p. 4.
The novel is a "horror story challenged by life." "After Cavan's death we are left, if not with a victory, at least with the rally of the human spirit in retreat." "... this novel concerns all who cherish intellectual and political freedom."

Synder, Marjorie. "Distinguished Book," Boston Herald, March 13, 1955, p. 4.
"Sarton's book is significant because it comes close to questions that trouble us all inwardly. Is it a crime to be liberal, intellectual, a believer in fundamental civil rights? Edward Cavan was all of these but, in the end, took his own life." ... "It is a beautifully designed and executed book, one to make thoughtful readers think."

United States Quarterly Book Review. 11 (June, 1955), 217.
"The form and style Sarton has given her material has grace and elegance." ... "The descriptions of academic life and the surroundings are well drawn, but the reader never really penetrates Cavan's personality because he is only seen through eyes of outsiders. One only really catches glimpses of him when he conducts his seminar class and in discussions with his 'spinster' friend."

Wagenknecht, Edward. "Look into 'Why Did He Do It?'," Chicago Tribune/Magazine of Books, March 13, 1955, p. 3.
This critic feels it may have been in bad taste for Sarton to write of Matthiessen's death (in the character of Cavan) so soon after the event, but she presents her hero admirably. "The book's didacticism keeps it from being very good." "The debate as to why Cavan committed suicide does not achieve the vividness of characterization or ... the brooding intensity of mood which is required to make the problem as moving as Sarton believes it is." Referring to the epilogue Wagenknecht writes, "... it is esthetically shocking in that it throws aside the objectivity of the book to present a heavily slanted account of a McCarthy like hearing. It was not necessary."

Weeks, Edward. "The Peripatetic Reviewer," Atlantic Monthly. 195 (May, 1955), 74.
Weeks calls this Sarton's best novel, partially due to the effect of Edward Cavan's suicide. He notes that even though the story parallels a tragedy that took place in Cambridge in 1950, the novel will be better appreciated by those who do not approach it as a book based on fact.

Wrong, Elaine. Canadian Forum. 35 (June, 1955), 70-71.

"This novel is a potpourri of assimilated political ideas woven into a plot presented in an interesting, time-structural way. Unfortunately, Cavan is almost a parody of a Hollywood neurotic personality. We are told he thinks great thoughts but we are never permitted to see any. The rest of the characters are paperdolls, unreal and thin-tissued." In Wrong's opinion the novel is cliche ridden and compared to Mary McCarthy's Groves of Academe, is like "... placing children's fiction on an adult shelf."

THE FUR PERSON, 1957

Beecroft, John. "A Gentleman Cat's Tale," New York Herald Tribune/Book Review, January 27, 1957, p. 9.
"I have read the book three times and looked into it several times more. Its charm increases." "People who are successful housekeepers for cats will see Sarton has understood the Cat who chose her."

Booklist and Subscription Books Bulletin. 53 (January 15, 1957), 246.
The book is briefly described as a humorous, unsentimental tale for cat lovers.

Bookmark. 16 (January, 1957), 86.
"Delicious story about a Gentleman Cat who becomes a Fur Person by deciding to stay with two, rare 'catly humans' as long as he lives."

Kirkus Review. 24 (November 5, 1956), 847.
The critic finds the book an "affectionate whimsy for a presumably always affectionate audience."

Lockridge, Richard. "Some Gentle Purrings," New York Times Book Review, January 20, 1957, p. 12.
"This book is an extremely pleasant example of the affinity between writers and cats and can hardly be improved upon--except perhaps by a less coy title. In Sarton's astute hands Tom is more the observer than the observed." "She has written a charming book."

M. L. "The Domestication of Tom," Saturday Review. 40 (February 2, 1957), 34.
"The author evidently believes Tom's situation to be immeasurably enhanced by these innovations (good

food, shelter, lavish attention) but it would be nice to have the cat's side of the story."

R. S. B. Springfield Republican, February 24, 1957, p. 8c.
"Sarton has directed her talents to a lively and instructive story about her cat. Like his distinguished mistress, Tom Jones the cat occasionally drops into poetry." "Cat fanciers will especially be attracted to this tale."

Wagenknecht, Edward. "Enduring New Cat Book," Chicago Sunday Tribune/Magazine of Books, January 20, 1957, p. 4.
"There are many passages in which Sarton attributes human emotions to Tom Jones, but she is not a nature fakir, for she always makes it clear that she is fooling. Her serious notation and description of cat behavior are keen indeed."

Willis, Katherine T. Library Journal. 82 (January 15, 1957), 193.
"What a joy it is to collect the fine creative geniuses of the world who can write delightful books about fine animals." "May Sarton's refined gift of story telling fits this Gentleman Cat."

THE BIRTH OF A GRANDFATHER, 1957

Balliett, Whitney. New Yorker. 33 (October 5, 1957), 194-197.
According to the critic this is Sarton's best novel, but it is not perfect. There are too many cliches in language; her prose lacks the sinew and tension that distinguish her best poetry. Finally, the novel bogs down into sentimentality at times.

Blackman, Ruth Chapman. "May Sarton's Proper Cantabrigians," Christian Science Monitor, September 12, 1957, p. 11.
"The men in the story suffer wordlessly, almost it seems subconsciously; whereas the women, with their great articulateness in such matters, constantly analyze." Blackman believes this novel cannot be considered one of Sarton's best. It lacks the dramatic conflict of Shadow of a Man; there is only occasionally an impression of "impressive writing."

Bookmark. 17 (October, 1957), 12.
"How Irish Tom Dorgon marries Betsy Wyeth, of a tightly knit New England clan, and brings fresh insight to detached Sprig, her father, is related in an interesting study of family relationships."

Butcher, Fanny. "Rare Satisfaction in Sarton Novel," Chicago Sunday Tribune, September 8, 1957, p. 5.
"This novel deals with the coming of age of a middle-aged man who has never really had to come to grips with life. Faced with two emotional crises, the knowledge that he is to become a grandfather, and the slow death of his most intimate friend, he must come to know himself or perish." ... "Sarton learned the art of writing by writing poetry. She writes with control, sense of a perfect fitting of the word to its use, the certainty that the right word is as important as the right idea, things which the restraints of writing poetry teach."

Hicks, Granville. "Some Good Fiction Which Won't Get the Popular Attention It Deserves," New Leader. 40 (October 7, 1957), 22.
"Sarton's work is a quiet novel but an enjoyable one, less dramatic than her Faithful Are the Wounds ... but distinguished by the same kind of insight." Hicks believes the unbelievable change in Sprig at the conclusion to be the weakest part of the book. He is shown only through the eyes of the other characters, a method which does not carry the reader to the core of his personality, and the change is not something the reader feels.

J. V. San Francisco Chronicle/This World, October 13, 1957, p. 22.
"Although there is restrained wit in it, this is a serious novel of family relationships, particularly about the shifts and changes that occur in families in the middle years." "Miss Sarton presents this period of transition ... with the sharp analysis of a skilled novelist and the emotions of a poet."

Janeway, Elizabeth. "Shifting Gears," New York Times Book Review, September 8, 1957, p. 4.
"This is a good book, but it could be better; The Shower of Summer Days was! The theme is serious and sensible and Sarton writes about it with sincerity

and accuracy, but it lacks force and a firm foundation." "The air of Cambridge and a third generation summer house is a little unfamiliar to most of us and Sarton's presentation is a little too oblique to make it understandable." "This is not a 'woman's novel' but the material is the feminine world of family and home. The delineation of the male characters is weak. Sarton needs to see her male characters in male terms, a task not impossible for a creative writer."

Keene, Francis. "Boston Excursion," Saturday Review. 40 (September 14, 1957), 49.

"This novel, like all her works, is civilized and unassumingly profound. Sarton's style is quiet, her dialogue true and sure. Her situations, though low-keyed are basic, alive with tension, drama and suspense. Her Anglo-Belgian origin gives Sarton the detachment necessary for dealing with people like the Wyeths."

Kelley, Mary. Library Journal. 82 (August, 1957), 1908.

"Flashes of emotional growth are fascinating because of the author's insight, and her ability to present situations in which most readers will find identification." "A family story that is well above average."

Kirkus Review. 25 (July 1, 1957), 455.

"Miss Sarton, whose talent is feminine, personal, deals again with delicate concerns and concepts--but certainly on occasion here her sensibility gives way to sentimentality. Not withstanding, many women will identify with it and enjoy it."

"New Fiction," The Times (London), March 27, 1958, p. 13.

"Her study of the emotional tension among a well-off family representing four generations taking a holiday on an island begins a trifle preciously--the island, psychologically and stylistically, lies somewhere between Virginia Woolf's lighthouse and Katherine Mansfield's bay--but her understanding of the characters involved develops, and her writing gains in power and imagination as the relationship between the differing age-groups are explored."

Stallings, Sylvia. "A Marriage That Survived Age and Crisis," New York Herald Tribune/Book Review, September 8, 1957, p. 3.

"The finest thing about May Sarton's book is its revelation that, as human beings worthy of the name, we never stop learning, never cease to explore the mysteries of this life in which human relationships are undoubtedly the greatest mystery of all."

Wilson, Angus. "Egoist-Idealist," The Observer (London), March 23, 1958, p. 16.

"It is in essence an American To the Lighthouse--a tracery of cultivated, self-aware, nuances of family relationships. As with Mrs. Woolf's famous novel, the trouble is that though everybody is highly sensitive to the moods of everyone else, they none of them know for a moment how smug and insulated they are in their gracious living.

THE SMALL ROOM, 1961

Butcher, Fanny. "A Tale of Forces of Thought at Work on the Campus," Chicago Sunday Tribune/Magazine of Books, August 20, 1961, p. 3.

"This novel is a book of atmosphere rather than events; a novel of ambience rather than actions." "The book doesn't sparkle, but it glows with warmth. It presents an honest picture of academic life."

Chapin, Louis. "Teachers Learning," Chiristian Science Monitor, August 24, 1961, p. 7.

"Sarton's penetrating enlightenment is at work in this novel. Her descriptions are vivid but the structural or conversational connections are not always clear." "But, it is a mature novel which deals with questions of honesty and integrity."

Emerson, Donald. Arizona Quarterly. 18 (Winter, 1962), 372-374.

"Without personal commitment there can be no true insight into the real work of a college. Sarton has this commitment and as a novelist of imagination and experience she has brought balance to the area of the academic novel. The main character, Lucy, learns painfully what it is to be a teacher. The small room is not only the classroom and her office but every one of the rooms in which Lucy's learning and teaching takes place--even all the rooms in which the essential life of the college takes place." Emerson sees this as one of the few academic novels which "reveals rather than exposes, shows rather than shows up."

Gannett, Lewis. "In This Grove All Is Not Pastoral," New York Herald Tribune/Books, August 20, 1961, p. 8.
"Sarton writes with a clarity akin to sunlight after a rain." "The essence of this novel is in the conflict of ideas rather than the conflict of characters." "Sarton makes considerable intellectual demands upon her readers."

Halley, Anne. "The Good Life in Recent Fiction," Massachusetts Review. 3 (Autumn, 1961), 192-193.
"The Small Room leaves one with the irritating sense of having read yet another Alumnae Bulletin puff about the good, grey professor...." The character of Lucy is "... not so much a heroine but a limited point of view. She is less than convincing because she commits herself to every college faction with sympathy." Halley contends that even though the novel asks many of the right questions about learning and teaching, the questions are all answered by the "off-stage help of the student plagiarist and the increased tea-time insights of the teachers."

Hogan, William. "Bookman's Notebook," San Francisco Chronicle, September 12, 1961, p. 33.
"Sarton works with stylish symplicity. Her performance in this novel is sustained, literate, perceptive and unfortunately dull."

Jackson, Katherine. "Books in Brief," Harper's Magazine. 223 (September, 1961), 102.
"What is the price of excellence?" is the over-riding question the novel poses, according to Jackson. Through the experience of one girl it is acted out in an absorbing and convincing charade. The book is full of ideas expounded in easy and amusing conversation." "A pleasant thought-provoking sojourn behind modern New England's ivied walls."

Janeway, Elizabeth. "The Responsible Ones," New York Times Book Review, August 20, 1961, p. 5.
"Sarton has chosen to write a serious novel about the serious work of a college and has brought it off with almost entire success. The only problem seems to be her protagonist and catalyst, Lucy Winter. She

is too much of a good thing. She is a new teacher and a novice yet she discovers the plagiarism of Jane and everyone ends up confiding in her." "But, the theme of the responsibility of the teacher to respond to her student's emotional needs as well as academic ones is superbly dealt with."

Kelley, Mary. Library Journal. 86 (September 1, 1961), 2820.

"This book is written with a depth and insight which comes from Sarton's teaching experience." "The novel will appeal to better women-readers, as well as everyone who has tried to teach."

Keown, Eric. "New Fiction," Punch. 242 (April 11, 1962), 586.

Keown compares The Small Room to some of the writing of C. P. Snow. "Both on the human and political levels Sarton makes this situation interesting and exciting."

Kiley, Frederick. "Halls of Ivy," Clearing House. 36 (April, 1962), 508.

"The Small Room represents an exact choice for the title of this novel, for the book hardly enlists sympathies from the inhabitants of the enormous room that some men call life." Following this statement, Kiley, attacks the book on every level: Lucy is called Pollyanna, she solves all the problems to everyone's satisfaction; Carryl Cope is described as "masculine"; Lucy's broken engagement is questioned, and Kiley suggests that it served only to prove that "... at one time Lucy might have resembled a woman."

Kirkus Review. 29 (June 15, 1961), 513.

This book tells a "... sympathetic story, graced with Sarton's fine drawn insights. Concerning itself with involvement, the novel asks, is teaching a creative impulse, a dedicated vocation or a refuge from the world for those who are emotionally stunted?"

McLaughlin, Richard. "The Small Room by Mary Sarton," Springfield Republican October 1, 1961, p. 4d.

"Despite a certain chilliness in writing, May Sarton ... has come up with a beautifully mature novel about life in a New England college." It not only limns the frustrations and tensions of the college's students and faculty but points up the antagonism that lies beneath teacher/student and teacher/teacher relationships."

McNiff, Mary. America. 105 (August 19, 1961), 638-639.
Reading this novel would "... help all appreciate the human elements invested, the conflicts and the cost involved in teaching." McNiff comments that she has read the book twice, "just for the joy of it."

Peterson, Virgilia. "Of Academic Conscience," Saturday Review. 44 (August 26, 1961), 18.
"Sarton speaks in muted notes but for those who listen this novel speaks with uncommon purity of pitch." Peterson praises her eloquent appraisal of teaching, noting Sarton possesses an "honorable mind."

Peterson, Virginia. "Briefly Noted Fiction," New Yorker. 38 (September 2, 1961), 77.
"This novel is absorbing but chilly. The vagueness of Lucy's love affair casts a shadow over the novel and weakens it." The critic comments that one cannot believe in her need for solitude and intensity of teaching if one doesn't know what lies behind it. "There is a sentimental air that hangs, faintly yet uneasily, over every encounter in the book."

Richardson, Maurice. "Owen Agonistes," New Statesman. 63 (April 6, 1962), 496.
Lucy is described by Richardson as an "insufferable prig!" and the college as having an atmosphere overcharged with hysteria and highmindedness. "... the plot is a little vamped up, the teaching staff seems to be more in need of a psychiatrist than the pupils."

Times Literary Supplement (London), March 30, 1962, p. 221.
"This novel is as just and scrupulous as a sonnet. One of the best of the many good things in this modest, satisfying book is Sarton's success in conveying the delight and excitement as well as the labour of teaching."

Weeks, Edward. "The Peripatetic Reader," Atlantic Monthly. 209 (January, 1962), 95.
"In this intense, perceptive story, the concise economy of Miss Sarton's style is a delight to read." "The power struggle for values is not described by Sarton in mere academese."

Wisconsin Library Bulletin. 57 (September/October, 1961), 308.

"May Sarton's writing adds distinction to an excellent story." "The unique relationship between teacher and student is explored."

JOANNA AND ULYSSES, 1962

Barrett, Mary. Library Journal. 88 (December 15, 1963), 4789.

"This gently realistic, mildly plaintive story is told in Sarton's quiet manner and might be a good one for young adults, or even for younger girls."

Bellows, Silence. "There Was a Donkey," Christian Science Monitor, December 5, 1963, p. 17.

"In Sarton's skillful hands the book is often amusing, always touching and significant. If ever a story ought to be true it is the story of Joanna and Ulysses."

Grunwald, Beverly. "Artist and Donkey," New York Times Book Review, November 24, 1963, p. 4.

"Compared to her other more serious fiction this book may be 'nothing.' It may be slight and occasionally sentimental but it is elegant and simple and has some good lines." "Sarton knows how to be tender, romantic, melancholic and amusing all at once."

Laski, M. New Statesman. 68 (November 13, 1964), 754.

"Joanna and Ulysses is perhaps an odd book to recommend to children since its heroine is a Greek woman who saves the life of a sick donkey, ..." "But the lessons novels do properly teach are lessons about what people are like, and what adults can be like is a lesson seldom taught to children in an acceptable fashion."

Maria Stella, Sister. Commonweal. 79 (December 6, 1963), 323.

"Sarton's way of seeing is poetic and uniquely her own."

Mudrick, Marvin. "Man Alive," Hudson Review. 17 (Spring, 1964), 110.

Mudrick reviews approximately twenty books in this article, Joanna and Ulysses being one among the many. He devotes two lines to this book, stating that it dramatizes the encounter of the "feminine sensibility with a charming little donkey."

Wagenknecht, Edward. "Instead of Sadism, a Gentle Touch," Chicago Tribune/Magazine of Books, November 24, 1963, p. 7.
"Few writers could have conceived and described, so convincingly, as Sarton does, the difficulties involved in caring for the donkey, Ulysses. This story presents tenderness without sentimentality and is a refreshing relief from the books filled with sex, violence and sadism."

Ware, Cade. "Briefly Noted Fiction," New Yorker. 39 (December 21, 1963), 95.
"Sarton tells this simple tale in a gently, unsentimental prose that is beautiful to read. A delightful, short novel."

________. "The Burros' Burden," Book Week. 1 (December 29, 1963), 11.
"Sarton is particularly adept at presenting intelligent women intelligently. Joanna is a fine addition to her gallery of portraits." "There is nothing that is not calm, light concernedly intelligent and well-formed in her work."

MRS. STEVENS HEARS THE MERMAIDS SINGING, 1965

Booklist and Subscription Books Bulletin. 62 (October 1, 1965), 141.
"With all her self-examination Hilary is careful not to see herself as a hedonist but to preserve the facade of a dedicated poet." "This novel is a well-written character study of a poet obsessed by her craft."

Brown, Ruth. "Magic Echoes and Mirrored Images," Saturday Review. 48 (October 23, 1965), 68.
"Sarton's writing is sensitive to the point of fussiness, and totally without humor." Brown sees Sarton's statements via Hilary as narcissistic. Her constant probing of Art is "... embarrassing because of its acute self-consciousness."

Chasin, Helen. "May Sarton," Village Voice. 19 (June 13, 1974), 36-38.
In this review of the 1974 edition of the novel,

Chasin views Mrs. Stevens as Sarton's mouthpiece, with no hint of irony. Hilary's voice is consistent with her role--she employs a "... public rhetorical tone and diction even in intimate moments." Hilary, according to Chasin, makes generalizations and pronouncements, particularly with regard to writing and women. "In the end, Sarton manifests her own complicity in the traditional oppressions and reinforces and perpetuates the damaging myths by encouraging women to be Eve ... to be Mary. The novel, with its special pleading and implicit self-justifying reads like a gloss of Sarton's life."

Corsini, Ray. "Down Memory Lane with Mrs. Stevens," New York Times Book Review, October 24, 1965, p. 53.

"Sarton has handled the theme, the mystery of the creative impulse, well. The plot is deceptively simple, the mood subtle, the feeling intense." "The music of Miss Sarton's prose leaves compelling echoes in one's mind."

Gardner, John. "An Invective against Mere Fiction," Southern Review. 3 (Spring, 1967), 454-455.

"Sarton is a careful craftsman with considerable intelligence, but she is shallow." "Mrs. Stevens is a self-pitying phony, an elderly lesbian and Sarton, for understandable reasons, can't see through her." "Great writing requires a great person to do the writing. Miss Sarton leaves us with fine craftsmanship and a trivial view of man and ... poetry."

Henderson, Joseph. "Initiation and the Psychology of Ego-Development in Adolescence," in Thresholds of Initiation. Connecticut: Wesleyan University Press, 1967, pp. 192-195.

Referring to Jung's writings on the process of initiation, Henderson views Sarton's novel as an "... instructive and beautifully written account of ... a therapeutic encounter...." He sees Hilary as the therapist and Mar as her mentor. Poetry can be seen as a "... creative openness toward the unconscious, with the intent to acquire self-knowledge." To Henderson Hilary represents Mar's anima-figure, and he, in turn, her animus-figure. "It is her eventual realization that he is ... her 'muse' that enables her to call forth the man ... in him as the wished-for liberation of her own creative talent, to become more mature than it had been...."

"In Brief," The Observer (London), March 6, 1966, p. 26.
The critic describes this as a novel in which an elderly female poet favors a couple of journalists with her life story and reflections on the Muse. "Evident sincerity of intentions is no compensation for a style in which sensibility is indistinguishable from self-indulgence."

Kirkus Review. 33 (July 1, 1965), 652.
"The tone of Hilary's rambling is adolescent, self-admiring and full of adroit self-justifications." The reviewer sees Hilary as justifying her lesbian loves as necessary to her art and is appalled by it. "In the hands of Colette this theme may have been written with irony, but in Sarton's hands, it is often simply embarrassing."

"Notes etc. on Books, etc.," Carleton Miscellaneous. 7 (Winter, 1966), 109.
"This is a finely contrived novel about Hilary Stevens, a poet in her seventies, who consents to an interview by two literary journalists intent upon discovering the sources of her inspiration. These sources and their revelation make the substance of the book."

Rennert, Maggie. "New Fiction," Book Week. 3 (October 24, 1965), 38.
Rennert criticizes Sarton for "... bruising English grammar and felicity as grievously as any Beatnik blow without offering either freshness of meaning or the thrill of rebellion." The critic contends that Doris Lessing's The Golden Notebook more adequately tells how it feels to be a woman and a writer than Mrs. Stevens....

________. "Briefly Noted Fiction," New Yorker. 41 (November 13, 1965), 246.
"Hilary is thoughtful, amiable and at times rueful. This is hardly a novel but a nice book, ..."

Shrapnel, Norman. Manchester Guardian. February 24, 1966, p. 11.
"To Sarton it seems the creative act is the result of being at home to the Muse--a visitor she actually

mentions by name--with occasional calls from minor angels or demons as well as interviewers." "The handling of her theme is over-sophisticated."

Shuttleworth, Martin. "New Fiction," Punch. 250 (February 23, 1966), 288.
"Sarton is no Colette, but she is a most painterly writer, honest, delicate and perceptive up to the snow-level of her mind...."

Taubman, Robert. New Statesman. 71 (February 18, 1966), 232.
"Mrs. Stevens ... has the would-be distinguished look of a novel that packs in more high seriousness than life. Sarton has a reputation in America much like Hilary's, a writer and personality of distinction but one wonders what the BBC would do with an interview with Sarton on her writing."

Thomas, William V. "Two Books from an Author Whose Audience May at Last Be Ready for Her," Washington, D.C. Star-News, September 1, 1974, n.p.
Examining the reissue of Mrs. Stevens ..., Thomas notes the welcomed new attention Sarton's fiction and poetry have begun to receive. "Yet in the case of this novel much of that attention has been shaded by feminist controversy over the political uses of art, which has had the unfortunate effect of directing focus away from the more profound qualities of the novel, that ideally should make it endure in our literature."

Thornton, Eugenia. "Novel Glorifies the Maturity of a Poetic Spirit," Plain Dealer (Cleveland), October 10, 1965, p. 7-H.
"... Miss Sarton has worked inward to accomplish a portrait of rich maturity of spirit whose gift to God has been acceptance of life and whose gift to the living has been love in all its many phases." "... she has given us a small classic; perfect in form, high in feeling, truth, and reverence for the best to be found in all things and all relationships."

Time. 86 (October 1, 1965), 126.
The critic views this novel as Sarton's excuse to review her own life through the eyes of Hilary. "Hilary gushes about lyrical art and Mar moons about his poetry and love for a sailor. Nothing else happens."

Times Literary Supplement (London). February 17, 1966, p. 128.

The plot consists of a layered series of flashbacks on the nature of passion and poetry. The critic wonders if Mrs. Stevens' justaposition with Mar, the aggressive and intellectual homosexual, is an image of her "animus." "... the form of the book is not viable; there are too many pronouncements of truths and the moments of real fiction occur too rarely."

Van Duyn, Mona. "The Poet as Novelist," Poetry. 109 (February, 1967), 333.

"This novel is vulnerable yet it is moving, it tells the truth if not convincingly about art, which may require more astringent expression, then at least about love, with a kind of brave disregard for the critical eye." Referring to the Lesbian theme, Van Duyn asks how Sarton could honestly write as a woman "... without having fully lived as a woman."

Willis, Katherine T. Library Journal. 90 (October 1, 1965) 4112.

Willis notes that this book is hard to review but not hard to read. "Sarton, like Hilary, is gifted, romantic, witty, intelligent, sensitive and a poet and novelist who realized that every past is the individual's own. This fine psychological study is for every fiction collection, but perhaps not in duplicate."

MISS PICKTHORN AND MR. HARE, 1966

Booklist and Subscription Books Bulletin. 63 (January 15, 1967), 522.

"A slight, pleasant story dealing with an overall attitude of graceful solicitude."

Butcher, Fanny. "Understanding Solitude," Chicago Sunday Tribune/Books Today, January 15, 1967, p. 4.

"Miss Pickthorn ... is a book of little surface importance, perhaps, but one which may be of much more impact to you than you suspect. It tells what solitude is, its urges and its twists of misunderstandings, its rewards and its dreams."

Choice. 4 (September, 1967), 676.

"This 'fable' would be interesting to students of

literature and creative writing." "Sarton's books, close to poetry, manage to both _mean_ and _be._"

Kirkus Review. 34 (September 15, 1966), 1011.
The reviewer calls this book "... a fable that comes close to being 'second-rate,' a goodhumored trifle which bookstalls may allow at Christmas."

Kitching, Jessie. _Publisher's Weekly._ 190 (October 10, 1966), 69.
"This is a delicate, slender book that offers remarkable insight into human nature. Sarton draws some surprising threads in this fable."

Malcolm, Janet. "Children's Books for Christmas," _New Yorker._ 42 (December 17, 1966), 220.
Malcolm reviews the book as a fable about the functions of poetry. "The development of Miss Pickthorn in the story is in a sense what happens to a person while reading a poem. He sees things in a different light." "The question that occupies the novelist (how shall we live?) is parried by the poet, whose subject is the fact that we all must die."

P. M. "Fiction in Brief," _Christian Science Monitor_, November 17, 1966, p. 14.
A short review: "A delightful, pleasantly old fable. Actually, it is a long short story rather than a novel."

Willis, Katherine T. _Library Journal._ 91 (November 1, 1966), 5431.
"This book is a landscape with figures both real and ideal." "Its pleasant psychology and quiet humor make it memorable."

THE POET AND THE DONKEY, 1969

"Briefly Noted Fiction," _New Yorker._ 45 (November 8, 1969), 206.
"This book is a small, sophisticated, elegantly sentimental journey through a New Hampshire village summer. The renewal of vitality of both the poet and the donkey is rewarding above and beyond the moral intended."

KINDS OF LOVE, 1970

"Books Briefly Noted," New Yorker. 46 (December, 1970), 143.

"With complete success Sarton portrays a small New Hampshire village held under a double spell--the spell cast by winter weather, and the spell of Christina's longing--a longing that continues to hold her story in tension after the ice and snow are gone and forgotten."

Halio, Jay. "First and Last Things," Southern Review. (Spring, 1973), 462-463.

Halio briefly mentions the novel in which he sees the main characters, Christina and Cornelius, as possessing a "gentleness and innate honorableness."

Meissner, Arolana. Library Journal. 95 (November 1, 1970), 3807.

"Sarton again proves her ability to weave plot and characterization into a fabric of artistic relationships. Her sympathy for the people and understanding of the places described add depth and realism to this new novel."

Murphy, James M., S. J. Best Sellers. 30 (December 1, 1970), 371.

Murphy sees this as more than a novel: "... at times it rises to the beauty which poetry alone can deliver. Love is shown mainly through Ellen Comstock and Christina Chapman. They are the essence of Willard."

Publishers Weekly. 201 (June 5, 1972), 141.

"Two lively and interesting older women begin this long and complex novel of life in a small New England town. The story is told in natural, easy style."

Rhodes, Richard. "How the Summer People Learned to Pass the Winter," New York Times Book Review, November 29, 1970, p. 56.

"This novel, flawed in style and flabby in content, is filled with characters but it does not bring the reader in to share the depth of their experiences. There is much potentially fascinating but Sarton leaves us on the outside. Perhaps the flaw is that she tells us of feelings rather than showing us. With the exception of Ellen Comstock the characters do not come alive." ... "It reads like a book intended for a private printing in the sense that Sarton assumes by her style that the reader already knows the people and events she portrays."

AS WE ARE NOW, 1973

Ackroyd, Peter. "Talking of Books," Spectator, July 27, 1974, 119.

Caro Spencer's reflections, according to Ackroyd, are conventional and her passion forbidding. "The conventional reflections were ruined for me when I realized that their source was a most unpleasant old party, being both boring and snobbish." He believes that Sarton does not seem to be aware of this but rather dwells on the "... fairest of all ... in her mirror."

Booklist and Subscription Books Bulletin. 70 (November 1, 1973), 278.

"This book is an honest and passionate journal of the way things are within institutional living."

Choice. 10 (January, 1974), 1722.

"The intention of the novel is admirable but unfortunately it borders on becoming a cliché. The reader has a sense of having seen or thought it all before." "The book is well written, and, for what it tries to do, is engrossing.

Coogan, Daniel. America. 130 (January 12, 1974), 16.

"This 'novella' is written with the utmost economy of style, reminiscent of Edith Wharton. Sarton has transfigured and illuminated by her art the bleak world for old age."

Douglas, Ellen. New York Times Book Review. November 4, 1973, p. 77.

"Sarton is an honest writer. She has created a convincing record of evil done and good intentions gone astray. The device of the journal kept by Caroline Spencer strengthens the book, it reinforces her isolation and helplessness and our guilt." But, Douglas faults Sarton for using too many clichés, which tend to "... dissipate the strong effects by use of intensive adverbs like 'rather,' 'really,' 'certainly,' 'very,' and 'awful.' In spite of these defects the novel is a powerful indictment."

Friedlander, Janet. Library Journal. 98 (August, 1973), 2338.
The main value of the book is its picture of the effects of institutionalization on individuals. The characters, although briefly sketched, are authentic. Caroline Spencer, emerges as a "... fully fleshed-out individual." "It is a well-written and easy to read novel."

Grumbach, Doris. "Fine Print," New Republic. 169 (October 13, 1973), 31.
"Everyone ought to read and live in this book for a while, especially the young. Sarton's book is fine fictional force, more devastating than de Beauvoir's The Coming of Age or Sharon Curtin's Nobody Ever Died of Old Age.

Kirkus Review. 41 (July 15, 1973), 773.
"May Sarton's novel ... is a law unto itself consisting always of sympathy, of old-fashioned poetic responses, of a woman true to her time while acknowledging how it has changed. In this novel (novella) the burden of sentiment is sharpened ... by anger. This is a small book as shocking as reality."

Marsh, Pamela. Christian Science Monitor. August 29, 1973, p. 9.
"Miss Sarton is a poet, writing with all the power of a poet, and her book will bring nightmares in the daytime to anyone reading it, unless we are prepared to take positive action about the horrible conditions she describes."

New Yorker. 50 (April 8, 1974), 141-142.
"Caroline Spencer is an opinionated, fiercely humane, lively woman, in this short novel. As the story progresses, she comes closer, emerging from the pages with a reality we can admire. She inspires care and love." "Miss Sarton has shown what a triumph a short novel can be."

Publishers Weekly. 204 (August 13, 1973), 44.
"The story is a fine, sensitive, honest look at the

dehumanization to which too many old people are subjected in badly run nursing homes." "Caro is a lovely, believable human being to whom the reader can really relate."

Rabinowitz, Dorothy. Saturday Review/World. 1 (September 11, 1973), 44.
"It is a bitter book, more a tract than a novel. But the work is a good piece of rhetoric. Sarton attempted to get inside a highly cultivated sensibility and has been successful. The book satisfied in a way that cold anger can when it is pure, despairing, and well written with no aim but the impulse to record the way things are."

Thwaite, Anthony. The Observer (London), July 28, 1974, p. 27.
"The trivial slights and the crueller deprivations of old age are woven together with complete authenticity." "Caro's orderly self-possession, her brisk humour, hopeless anger, fear, tenderness, strength, are all built up with a straightforwardness of address that is a small triumph of characterisation." On a critical note, Thwaite sees the novel's ending as a "melodrama, a bit too willed and neat."

Times Literary Supplement. "Notes from Purgatory," August 9, 1974, p. 849.
"May Sarton suggests wonderfully the fears of the old in this diary of a woman proud, discreet and determined to die intact. The writing itself is tense with the exertions of a brave, doomed battle against inner collapse; the prose, which struggles to be lucid, provides a truth, pessimistic at best, which relates how impossible it is to help people to relinquish what has been important to them in their lives. For this reason it is clear that Caro's final panic, bitterness and self-immolation was inevitable."

PUNCH'S SECRET, 1974

Booklist and Subscription Books Bulletin. 70 (May 15, 1974), 1059.
"A pleasant, quiet book written smoothly in free verse. The poetry borders on insignificance but is redeemed by the author's sensitivity to animal nature and childlike anthropomorphizing."

French, Janet. Library Journal. 99 (September, 1974), 2255.

"Spare, rhythmic free verse ... in which the theme of loneliness and hoped for friendship is one that children will understand ..."

Kirkus Review. 42 (April 1, 1974), 361.

"The accent of 'Joy' and the particularized observations of Punch perk up [Sarton's] latest attempt to deal in a gentle/minimum of words with a small creature finding someone to love."

Martin, Patricia Miles. "Pat Scans the Junior Bookshelf," Palo Alto Times. Peninsula Living, February 8, 1975, p. 19.

"Punch's Secret is exquisite yet simply written. Sarton's solution to Punch's loneliness is unexpected and perfect."

Publishers Weekly. 205 (March 18, 1974), 52.

"Sarton's style and Knott's handsome illustrations make the book rise above its rather mundane parts. Punch is so vain he borders on the egomaniacal."

Wetzsteon, Ross. New York Times Book Review, September 1, 1974, p. 8.

The critic finds the book, after a second reading, disturbing and frightening. "Punch does not really reveal his secret in the end. There is something unconvincingly passive about Sarton's conception of Punch, something unacceptably accepting. Punch would really like to escape from his confining cage. His dream is not so much of 'someone to love' but of flapping his wings and rising swiftly above the treetops, screaming against the sky."

CRUCIAL CONVERSATION, 1975

Grumbach, Doris. New York Times Book Review, April 27, 1975, p. 4.

"... the three protagonists are all at an age of rigidity ... so their crucial conversations with each other, in a series of somewhat automatic, sometimes synthetic closet scenes, produce no light between the talkers, only great heat." The light that does result "... produces insight for the reader into the modern dilemma of freedom vs. marriage, self-realization vs. service and duty...." Grumbach believes this is not Sarton's best novel. "It is not prime Sarton, but then we are still waiting for what we have always expected she would do some day and has not yet quite done. Her work gives us the sense of the perpetually promising...." But the novel is moving and, for Sarton, represents a new step forward by suggesting a "radical solution to the human-bondage-in-marriage status."

Kameen, Paul. Best Sellers. 35 (July, 1975), 91.
"There's a little Watergate, a little Vietnam, a little of everything in fact. But characters that are too stiff to come to life, engaging in conversations that don't even come close to ringing true, can't offer much support to a story-line that's already badly frayed from overuse."

Keating, H. R. F. The Times (London), January 8, 1976, n. p.
Calling the novel "disciplined and gracefully brief," Keating praises Sarton's handling of a currently popular theme. "... the ideas and central debate in Crucial Conversations matter, lastingly to everyone, and a link between an energetic conscious in public and in domestic life is made with refreshing clarity."

Kirkus Review. 63 (March 1, 1975), 261.
This novel lacks the urgency of the issue of her last one (As We Are Now). The situation is common enough: Poppy, fifty, decides to leave her husband of twenty-seven years to search for her "personhood." It is not so much the women's movement which has brought home to her the "sullying business of compromise," but rather the incidences of Watergate. She realizes that she is still a "terribly unfinished, searching mass of conflict." "That's about it--a domestic sundry and no doubt Miss Sarton's readership, an unquestionably steadfast one, will not reproach her for what seems less than authentic...."

Lehmann-Haupt, Christopher. New York Times, June 16, 1975, p. 25.
"Crucial Conversations is an ideal scenario for dramatizing the efficacy of the women's liberation movement. Everyone has perfect arguments to present ... everything is perfectly balanced--the case for individual

freedom against that for family responsibility; the weight of public events ... against the private incidents that have corroded the marriage. The only trouble is that ... it doesn't count for a thing, because no real person was ever so uncompromising and articulate and morally self-conscious as Miss Sarton's characters are."

Powell, Judith W. Library Journal. 100 (June 15, 1975), 1242.

"It is a woman's story as viewed through a man's conversations...." "His sensitivity to the nuances of the relationship and his own pain and resulting growth are what give this story added dimension and depth of perception not seen elsewhere in recent women's fiction."

Publishers Weekly. 207 (March 31, 1975), 42.

"... this is not so much a novel as a psychological probing of the innermost emotional secrets of husband, wife and friend." ... "Ms. Sarton explores thoughtfully the desperation many women feel in supposedly 'contented' situations and makes Poppy's valiant perversity perfectly understandable."

Weeks, Edward. "The Peripatetic Reviewer," Atlantic Monthly. 235 (June, 1975), 93-94.

"Miss Sarton is usually best in her portraits of women, and Poppy ... is altogether believable. The interfering bachelor, Pip, has a feminine streak in him." ... "The desire of a woman who has been suffocated in her marriage to be true to herself in the last third of her life is very much a reality and no longer considered a scandal in our society. The wonder is that Poppy waited so long."

A WALK THROUGH THE WOODS, 1976

Chatfield, Carol. School Library Journal. 22 (March, 1976), 97.

"A special book for quiet times, for cat and dog lovers, and for readers with imagination." "The text is concise, and the pastel illustrations hint at the scene, leaving reader's imagination to fill in the rest. While the unhurried pace and style won't appeal to everyone, it's a very pleasant stroll for kindred spirits."

Publishers Weekly. 209 (February 23, 1976), 120.

It is noon and the poet, who has been writing at her desk all morning, decides it's time for a walk. Tamas her dog and Bramble her cat join the poet in the hike through the woods. "As for the poet, she knows how ... to persuade her audience to share with her not only the bracing walk, but the treasures it brings her; 'an emerald cushion of moss ... the lady-slipper, a secret treasure!' "

BOOK REVIEWS / NON-FICTION

I KNEW A PHOENIX, 1959

Bacon, Martha. "Gone with the War," Saturday Review. 42 (May 2, 1959), 39-40.

Bacon recounts the highlights of this work: "The chapters of the book are indeed sketches, finely limned and gracefully illuminated. While Miss Sarton talks to us we feel as though we were working through a cultivated landscape in the early afternoon of a summer's day, with twilight far in the future."

Blackman, Ruth. "A Writer Self-Observed," Christian Science Monitor, April 30, 1959, p. 11.

"Sarton conveys her unique experience in a style straightforward yet evocative, with a cadence that seems inevitable, but like the cadence of good poetry, is not. Her sketches are suffused with the light and color of poetry. Always there is a sense of becoming oneself."

Booklist and Subscription Books Bulletin. 55 (May, 1959), 505.

"Witty, nostalgic, and literate memories for the discriminating reader."

Bookmark. 18 (April, 1959), 173.

"Early memories of Sarton's parents, schooling, theatrical and literary apprenticeship make up the substance of the beautifully written chapters in this book."

Hughes, David. "Three Writers in the Making," The Sunday Times (London), February 24, 1963, p. 28.

I Knew a Phoenix, a book of solemn charm and great accuracy of perception, is really an accumulation of the glimpses and insights that went into the making of a poet. "She succeeds in turning the stuff of poems into a brisk narrative and the rhythms of poetry into a prose that is soft of tone, rich in texture, and always impishly surprising."

Humble, Christopher. The Listener. 69 (April 11, 1936), 642.

"Sarton has a clear, straightforward style, is never enthralling. She harkens back, delicately yet with common sense. She is not guilty of the usual snares of feminine reminiscence."

Hutchens, John K. New York Herald Tribune, April 28, 1959, p. 21.

"Sketches for an autobiography Miss Sarton reticently subtitles these charming vignettes of her origin and herself, but it would be hard to imagine their special quality improved by greater length or more detail. For they tell us, with a finality of their own, how it happened that two firmly rooted Europeans quite suddenly found themselves in another world, and what went into the making of an American, their daughter."

Kirkus Review. 27 (February 15, 1959), 171.

"A vivid and nostalgic evocation of people moving in the places of memories past." ... "A book touched with the magic of an imaginative and grateful heart."

McLaughlin, Richard. "Career Sketched by Poet-Novelist," Springfield Republican, July 5, 1959, p. 4d.

"Alive with [Sarton's] poetic imagery, these sketches for an autobiography are engaging. Her indebtedness to such creative artists as Julian Huxley, Elizabeth Bowen, S. S. Kotelianisky and Virginia Woolf had a maturing effect on Sarton as a creative writer."

Peterson, Virgilia. New York Herald Tribune/Book Review, April 26, 1959, p. 3.

"This book is not so much about Sarton as it is a mirror to refract the very special lights that lit her path to maturity. The story of her individuality is rare in a time when commercial anonymity is threatening to engulf us. Sarton has the eye and the ear and the instinct to recognize beauty wherever she finds it. She has known many phoenixes and in her humility and wonder before life, she is something of a phoenix herself."

Pippett, Aileen. "Lives Seen in a Flash," New York Times Book Review, June 28, 1959, p. 4.
"Above and beyond the facts and dates marking the turning points in the education of a writer, every chapter is illuminated by the poet's vision of life, the response of an ardent mind and a generous heart."

Scratton, Mary. "A Luminous Veil," Times Literary Supplement, August 9, 1963, p. 607.
"Sarton writes with a style and vision associated with the belles lettres of the 1890's and Richard le Gallienne, whose daughter became Sarton's theatrical mentor. It is exquisite, poised writing but sometimes close to nostalgia." "But, by the grace of her enthusiasm and penetration, her palate for flavors, her ability to squeeze essence from its hulk of harshness, it becomes in the end a clear, honest vision."

Voiles, Jane. San Francisco Chronicle/This World, May 3, 1959, p. 27.
"In crisp, firm writing Sarton fulfills Elizabeth Bowen's precepts of writing autobiography: disciplined concentration and the 'I' provide fresh perception of everything told. Sarton searches for the essence rather than the details of places and personalities. It is not romantic nostalgia but a hard core of discipline."

Wagenknecht, Edward. "Gleams and Glimpses into Life of a Writer," Chicago Sunday Tribune/Magazine of Books, April 26, 1959, p. 6.
"The book is a collection of autobiographical fragments rather than an autobiography." "The first section, about her parents, is charming but could have been filled out into more than just glimpses."

Willis, Katherine. Library Journal. 84 (April 1, 1959), 1125.
"Sarton gives us a charming bit of autobiography. For the pleasure of reading, this is to be recommended."

Wisconsin Library Bulletin. 55 (May/June, 1959), 254.
"Patrons who are acquainted with the Sarton name will be eager for this book; others should be introduced to it."

PLANT DREAMING DEEP, 1968

American Notes and Queries. 6 (May, 1968), 141.

"Plant ... is an opening of the poet's heart reflecting on the turning year inside and outside of a rural New Hampshire home filled with a crowded solitude of countrified moods."

Atkinson, Brooks. New York Times Book Review, February 4, 1968, p. 39.

"In this sensitive, luminous book Sarton writes of her house which reflects her tastes and style--immaculate and orderly, traditional, basically austere with overtones of grace and charm." "There is pain in her book and two demons continue to possess her: the demon that argued since she was born in Europe she was not equipped to write novels with American themes; and the demon that as a writer she is not recognized and that literary critics stand between her and her public." "But there are also joys in this book--gardens, solitude, special friends. Love is the genius of this small but tender and often poignant book by a woman of many insights."

Booklist and Subscription Books Bulletin. 64 (May 1, 1968), 1018.

The reviewer sees Plant ... as a prose accompaniment to As Does New Hampshire, in which she "amplifies her discourse writing, friends, gardening and the meaningful life."

Hicks, Granville. "The Advantages of Country Living," Saturday Review. 51 (February 17, 1968), 27-28.

"Plant ... is tenderly poetic though not sentimental." "It is a well wrought book about a woman living alone, her work as a writer, and her experiences in life."

Irving, Maggie. "Woman in the House," The Boston Globe, March 11, 1968, p. 19.

Irving notes that for Sarton, learning to live alone in the house she bought was a matter of heavy personal involvement. "The line between solitude, self-chosen, and loneliness is hair-fine, and can be breached at any moment." The heart of Plant ... is Sarton's gift of capturing the essence of something, somewhere or someone; these essences are "... distilled from a life tethered to the self-imposed pressures, the discouragements and satisfactions of writing, as well as the pleasures of existence."

Ruffin, Carolyn. "A Poet and Her Home Building," Christian Science Monitor, April 4, 1969, p. 19.

"This book is a biography of a house and an autobiography of a mind. The house is a place for accenting just the right poet-concepts of solitude and isolation." "But, the book lacks compactness; not everything is integrated or 'falls into place' for the reader as it does for Sarton and this tends to make it overburdened.

Willis, Katherine T. Library Journal. 92 (December 15, 1967), 4498.

"Sarton shows a growing creative genius and an easy style as she analyzes herself and her 'intangibles (life and thought, fears and demons, and rewards),' and her tangibles (friends, events, weather, and her house)."

JOURNAL OF A SOLITUDE, 1973

Booklist and Subscription Books Bulletin. 69 (July 15, 1973), 1045.

"Sarton's journal penetrates deep into the human spirit and reveals the necessity of accepting pain. Throughout, she conveys a sense of self that may strike responsive chords in persons seeking to come to terms with their own lives."

Choice. 10 (September, 1973), 984.

"Journal ... reveals a different Sarton from Plant ... or Kinds of Love; the person revealed is closer to Hilary Stevens. She honestly and painfully records her anguish, loneliness and spiritual conflict. Journal ... will come as a surprise to those readers who romanticized her and failed to note the signs of fire."

Ferrari, Margaret. "Women: Medieval and Modern War: Politics and Death," America. 129 (September 1, 1973), 126.

"The self-examination in Journal ... is engrossing self-revelation. Sarton is skeptical about romantic love. She worries about death, she confronts and learns from anger. She treats it in the past tense, after it has been subdued. This journal reveals an interesting personality tension: an openness to new people and ideas, and a passion for order and control which would seem to limit spontaneity and enthusiasm. It offers convincing and intimate contact with a middle-aged woman's 'dark night of the soul'."

Gellatly, Peter. Library Journal. 98 (April 1, 1973), 1157.
"The reader learns what it's like for Sarton to inhabit her own skin. This personal testimony is a valuable continuation to the anatomy of the creative process."

Gregory Duffy, Sister. Best Sellers. 33 (June 1, 1973), 121.
"Journal ... is an honest and beautiful book. Few persons possess her wisdom, passion and understanding; fewer still are capable of communicating ideas in such effortless, cadenced prose."

Meras, Phyllis. "Journeying through the Countryside," New York Times Book Review, May 13, 1973, p. 14.
"Sarton is more of a poet/philosopher than a naturalist, and her references to flowers and seasons are backdrops and atmosphere for the agony of fading love, sorrow at the death of a friend, fatigue after the poetic process and the need for aloneness. Sometimes her attempt to exorcise troubled emotions seems mannered and excessive." "There is too much intensity."

Publishers Weekly. 203 (February 19, 1973), 77.
"This book is honest to the point of bluntness, especially evocative as well in her descriptions of the New Hampshire farmhouse where she makes her home, she conveys a sense of self. At times ... she seems very like Colette, although her books are flavored with New England rather than Europe." "Journal ... is a reassessment of her life and work."

A WORLD OF LIGHT, 1976

Bell, Pearl K. "May Sarton: Friendships that Flowered," New York Times Book Review, October 3, 1976, pp. 6-7, 18.
Bell believes that the most absorbing portraits in

A World of Light are those of well-known writers, particularly Elizabeth Bowen and Louise Bogan. "Yet neither of these tragically complex writers, though their portraits are the most ambitious and outspoken in the book, comes sufficiently into focus, because Miss Sarton tends to be overly fond of sentimental and ardently vague generalities." Bell also accuses Sarton of lifting "large chunks ... with scarcely a word altered" from her earlier autobiographical writings and consequently does not bring new judgment and feeling to the present book. "A World of Light makes it clear that, ... four volumes of autobiographical reminiscences and self-exploring memoir have been more than enough."

Hodgson, Eleanor. "All Sorts of People Came into May Sarton's World," San Francisco Examiner and Chronicle World, November 4, 1976, p. 34.

"The lives of all of us are intertwined with others but rarely with all the passionate intensity that ... May Sarton brings to her relationships." "The book (A World of Light) is a beautifully written work of a mature woman, witty, warm and wise."

ANNOTATED BIOGRAPHICAL/CRITICAL ARTICLES

Anderson, Dawn Holt. "May Sarton's Women," Images of Women in Fiction. Ed. Susan K. Cornillon. Ohio: Bowling Green University Popular Press, 1972, 243-250.

This chapter explores the women characters created by Sarton as examples of unique, fulfilled individuals. "Miss Sarton examines valid relationships that women can form, especially with other women, which are outside the usual relationships available to them--women talking, playing and creating together meaningfully." Anderson discusses Sarton's books Joanna and Ulysses, The Small Room and Mrs. Stevens Hears the Mermaids Singing in terms of this concept. Sarton's characters exemplify the pattern of life, of a woman alone, learning through her relationships with others to make full use of her own creative talents." Anderson notes that the idea for her essay was derived from an unpublished paper by Susan Cornillon.

Bakerman, Jane S. "May Sarton's 'The Small Room': A Comparison and an Analysis," Chrysallis Journal. 1 (Summer, 1975), 36-47 [orig. was unpub. paper--see p155].

Bakerman discusses Sarton's novel The Small Room in relationship to several other of Sarton's works, specifically I Knew a Phoenix and Faithful Are the Wounds. According to the critic The Small Room is a "... major American novel, too often overlooked by critics." "Its themes, the importance of teaching, the question of head vs. heart, and isolation, provide the driving force for the novels [sic] I Knew a Phoenix and Faithful...." Bakerman views the novel's setting and the characters' experiences as a microcosm. "The novel as a whole examines the price one pays for the excellence of an honest mind and the pain envy causes in a close community. Redemptive suffering and merciful justice provide the workable answer." "... The

Small Room is a work of magnitude and ... it develops further major themes in Sarton's novels, which deserve more critical attention."

Bannon, Barbara A. "May Sarton," Publishers Weekly. 205 (June 24, 1974), 25.

This article is an interview with May Sarton upon the publication of the collected volume of her poems (Collected Poems 1930-1973) and the publication of a new edition of Mrs. Stevens Hears the Mermaids Singing. Sarton comments: "I try to live as if every moment of life is eternal." She talks about her writing, both poetry and novels, and her need for solitude but recognition as well, and the sustaining force her readers have been to her.

Barkham, John. "The Private World of a New England Poet-Novelist," San Francisco Chronicle/This World, June 19, 1966, p. 43.

Barkham, in his description of Sarton's life and work in Nelson, New Hampshire, writes that living alone had not made her a recluse. "... her conversation is lively, even vivacious, and she talks readily and eloquently of her home and her writing." Barkham touches on such areas as Sarton's attitude about her writing (both poetry and fiction) the place of the female writer in the literary world, and her own solitary life. "I could live alone indefinitely and feel no need for company. Solitude can be very exciting."

Drewes, Caroline. "A Radical Feminist with a Quiet Voice," San Francisco Examiner, November 29, 1976, p. 25.

May Sarton, now 64, is a woman who has lived alone, successfully, for many years, addressing herself to her private demons and to such philosophic matters as solitude, friendship, love and inevitably, old age. Most recently she has become a symbol to feminists, "... a role model for women looking for role models," she notes. Discussing her homosexuality as expressed in the novel Mrs. Stevens Hears the Mermaids Singing, Sarton comments, "I have been trying to say radical things gently so that they may penetrate without shock." Summing up her personal philosophy, "I try to live as if every day, might be my last, and yet, is eternal. You can only do this well in solitude."

Grumbach, Doris. "The Long Solitude of May Sarton," The New Republic. 170 (June 8, 1974), 31-32.
Grumbach admits that she admires the nature of Sarton's career--"serene-seeming despite her declared traumas." Noting that everything she has written is solid yet sensitive, Grumbach draws together her philosophy. "Hers has been a durable fire, despite the fact that criticism and recognition have often ignored her; her small room seems to make most male critics uncomfortable."

Hammel, Lisa. "'There ... Stood the House'," New York Times Magazine, August 23, 1970, pp. 50-51.
This article is a photographic essay of Sarton's house in Nelson, New Hampshire, interspersed with quotations from her book Plant Dreaming Deep.

Jones, Llewellyn. "Poets in Epitome," The Universalist Leader, June, 1958, pp. 139-140.
Jones notes that Sarton is to America about what, forty years ago, John Galsworthy was to Great Britain. He adds, this judgment is "merely topographical, not literary." In her poetry, according to Jones, Sarton expresses the total personality. "Sarton's appreciation of texture, color, the pictorial, the musical, is immediately integrated into a feeling of order and discipline."

Martin, Lucy L. "May Sarton: Poetry (Life) Is a Discipline Not a Self-Indulgence," Maine Times, June 20, 1975, pp. 22-23.
At sixty-two Sarton still believes that, as a whole, the critics have ignored her. She is more well known today than in the past but still does not have a "reputable place in college anthologies." She compares her books to Flemish painters "... whose bold brushstrokes make clear the troubled humanity in a face ..." Her intention is to enhance life, not sentimentalize it. Martin suggests that Sarton's neglect may be due to her views on love and sex--love as a kind of "heroic inner demand," and the lack of explicit sexuality in her works. Sarton believes her novel Mrs. Stevens Hears the Mermaids Singing to be a key work: "I've never written a book that's had so great an impact." In this novel the author identifies Hilary Stevens' (the main character) source of inspiration to be women.

In concluding the article Sarton talks about her current attitude toward her life: her satisfaction has come "partly with age, with accepting myself, no longer having so much conflict, and seeing the good things about getting old." The current recognition of her work has helped. She has grown to accept herself, and her achievements.

Norman, Anne. "Writer's Secrets Shared," Los Angeles Times, March 16, 1957, p. 6.

Giving advice to the would-be writer Sarton comments: "Writers must expect to spend years of training to be successful. I can't understand why young people accept the fact that years of training are needed to develop a successful violinist but expect a writer to achieve success without determination and discipline." Poetry is very exacting but rewarding, notes Sarton. "You cannot write a poem by just wanting to. A poem usually starts with a single line which floats up into the mind ..." "From there it takes about twenty rewrites before it is completed." "I feel that a writer is a screen through which life passes and is transmitted to others."

Putney, Paula. "Sister of the Mirage and Echo," Contempora. 2 (Spring, 1972), 1-6.

Putney's overall theme in this interview with Sarton is the battle which a woman must endure to succeed as a professional writer. The woman who needs to create works of art is born with a kind of "psychic tension" in her which drives her to find balance, to make herself whole, according to Sarton. "A woman artist fulfills this need at the expense of herself as a woman." Discussing the concept of form, Sarton equates it with freedom. A routine which looks confining is actually what frees one. Form, in poetry, gives solidarity and transparency. Overall, Sarton's view of writing has been an intellectual approach to feeling. In her mature works intellect and feeling are balanced.

Rule, Jane. "May Sarton," Lesbian Images. New York: Doubleday & Co., Inc., 1975, 164-174.

In her chapter on May Sarton, Rule believes that Sarton labors under a double guilt: "... not only does she want to be left alone to get on with her writing but she would also like to cast another in the role of listener which she so passionately rejects, and therefore she knows in herself the pain of that rejection." Rule contends that Sarton also fears being "distorted" by readers because of the homosexual theme in her works. Becuase of this it took courage for her to write the novel Mrs. Stevens.... Rule faults Sarton for relying too heavily on Freudian interpretations for human behavior, "... this makes her call a great many needs and strengths which are simply human either masculine or feminine instead." But, Sarton has not become a pseudo-man to solve the problem of dealing with sex in her writing: "... she has too much respect for women to set herself so much apart from them."

Sibley, Agnes. May Sarton. New York: Twayne Publishers, 1972.

In her preface Sibley writes that this book undertakes to show the unity of all Sarton's writing. The first chapter summarizes her life, the second discusses her poems and ideas about the nature of poetry as she has given them in articles, lectures and novels, the third and fourth deal with her novels, and the last summarizes the chief themes that have been set forth and evaluates her achievement as a writer. This work includes a selected bibliography and index.

Taves, Isabella. "Alone Does Not Mean Lonely," San Jose News, August 13, 1974, p. 22.

In an article discussing the difference between solitude and loneliness, Taves quotes Sarton ("a wonderful poet and novelist") "Solitude is the salt of personhood." Taves further quotes from an article Sarton wrote for the New York Times entitled "The Rewards of Living a Solitary Life."

West, Paul. "Time, South and Indentity," The Modern Novel. Vol. 2. London: Hutchinson University Library, 1965.

West discusses the modern novelist's persistence to "... espouse modern America." "The intellectual novelists--from May Sarton (A Shower of Summer Days; Faithful are the Wounds) and Trilling to Mary McCarthy and Harvey Swados--converse among themselves.

What the Woman Lived: Selected Letters of Louise Bogan, 1920-1970. Ed. Ruth Limmer. New York: Harcourt Brace Jovanovich, 1973.

This work contains several letters to May Sarton from Bogan, many of them referring to Sarton's poetry. Remarking on the sonnet sequence in _Cloud, Stone, Sun, Vine_, Bogan does not believe that this type of sequence can be written in our century, especially by women, without becoming "discursive." Again, Bogan notes that Sarton should have ended the sequence with an "unresolved positive anger" rather than a questioning acceptance. Writing to Sarton about lyric poetry in general she states, "... there must be an element of wit, there is nothing duller or more unmalleable than serious conviction, seriously expressed."

UNPUBLISHED PAPERS

(Modern Language Association)

Anderson, L. W. "May Sarton's Liberated Women," Ohio: Bowling Green State University, 1973.

Bakerman, Jane S. "Kinds of Love: Patterns of Love and Friendship in Five Novels by May Sarton," Indiana: Indiana State University, 1974.

________. "May Sarton's The Small Room: A Comparison and an Analysis," Indiana: Indiana State University, 1973 [published in 1975--see p149].

________. "Perimeters of Power: An Examination of As We Are Now," Indiana: Indiana State University, 1974.

Bartz, Fredrica. "A Private Room: Image and Theme in May Sarton's Mrs. Stevens Hears the Mermaids Singing," Michigan: University of Michigan, 1973.

Bryan, Mary. "Rage for Justice: Political, Social and Moral Consciousness in Selected Novels of May Sarton," Massachusetts: Regis College, 1974.

Cannon, Melissa. "The Barriers of Self and the Test of Love: A Dialogue for Two Voices," 1973.

Cleveland, Carol L. "Outclassed in America: Two Novels about the Old," New York: University of Buffalo, 1975.

Connelly, Maureen. "Death and Love: The Eternal Equation: The Sonnets of May Sarton," Massachusetts: Boston State College, 1975.

________. "Metaphor in Five Garden Poems by May Sarton," Massachusetts: Boston State College, 1974.

Eddy, Darlene M. "The Sculptor and the Rock: Some uses of Myth in the Poetry of May Sarton," Indiana: Ball State University, 1975.

Fowler, Sigrid H. "May Sarton and the Balance," Pennsylvania: State College of Pennsylvania, 1973.

________. "A Note on May Sarton's Use of Form," Pennsylvania: State College of Pennsylvania, 1974.

Frank, Charles. "May Sarton's Autobiographical Trilogy," Illinois: Illinois College, 1973.

Hauser, Susan. "A Durable Fire: New Poems, by May Sarton: A Descriptive Review," Ohio: Bowling Green State University, 1973.

Klein, Kathleen. "Myth Destroyed," 1973.

________. "To Grow Old and Die," Indiana: Indiana University-Purdue University, 1975.

Lupton, Mary Jane. "Solitude a Deux: May Sarton and the Journal Form," Maryland: Morgan State College, 1974.

Lydon, Mary. "A French Scholar's Feminist View of May Sarton," Wisconsin: University of Wisconsin, 1975.

Osborne, Nancy. "The Literature of Generativity: May Sarton's Journal of a Solitude," New York: Syracuse University, 1974.

Putney, Paula G. "The Structure Within," Georgia: Atlanta, 1973.

Taylor, Henry. "The Singing Wound: Intensifying Paradoxes in May Sarton's 'A Divorce of Lovers'," Washington, D.C.: American University, 1973.

Wortham, Thomas. "'Teach me to heare Mermaids singing': Sacred and Profane Love in the Novels of May Sarton," California: University of California/Los Angeles, 1975.

MISCELLANEA

Carlsen, Robert, Tony Manna and Betty Lou Tucker. "Books for Young Adults: 1974 Honor Listing," English Journal. 64, (January, 1975), 112-115.

Books which appear on this list are chosen by older high school students. The aim is to note those books which prove most popular. Under the heading "Positive Values" are included books which concern man and his values; As We Are Now by May Sarton was listed in this category.

Cotter, James Finn. "Women Poets: Malign Neglect?" America. 128 (February 17, 1973), 140-142.

May Sarton's name is listed among other women poets such as Phyllis McGinley, Josephine Miles, et al. as being all but absent from major poetry anthologies. Cotter believes they all "... wrote poems worthy of a wider audience."

Harrison, Barbara G. "A Troubled Peace," MS. 3 (November, 1974), 40, 46, 93-94, 96.

In this review of the selected letters of Louise Bogan, May Sarton is mentioned as one of her correspondents.

Henry, Richard. Composing a Life: A Celebration Based on the Work of May Sarton. Massachusetts: Religious Art Guild, 1974.

This work is a combination of selected readings from Sarton's writing with musical selections interspersed.

Justus, James H. "Fiction: The 1930's to the Present," American Literary Scholarship: An Annual/1972. Ed. J. Albert Robbins. North Carolina: Duke University Press, 1974, pp. 310-311.

There is a brief mention of Agnes Sibley's book on May Sarton as a straightforward and useful introduction to Sarton's poetry and fiction. Of Dawn Anderson's essay, "May Sarton's Women" Justus writes "... it characterizes them as models who require solitude for realizing their own identities." Anderson, according to Justus, believes that Sarton regards sexual relationships as 'debilitating' to personal growth.

Medzger, Betty. Women at Work: A Photographic Documentary. New York: Sheed and Ward, Inc., 1975, pp. 58-59.

An excerpt from Mrs. Stevens Hears the Mermaids Singing accompanies a photograph of May Sarton taken in her study at York, Maine.

APPENDIX:

PARTIAL CHECKLIST OF INDIVIDUAL POEMS

KEY TO ABBREVIATIONS

ADNH	As Does New Hampshire, Sarton, 1967.
CP	Collected Poems, 1930-1973, Sarton, 1974.
CSSV	Cloud, Stone, Sun, Vine, Sarton, 1961.
DF	A Durable Fire, Sarton, 1972.
EiA	Encounter in April, Sarton, 1937.
GoMS	A Grain of Mustard Seed, Sarton, 1971.
IL	Inner Landscape, Sarton, 1939.
ITLA	In Time Like Air, Sarton, 1958.
LoS	Land of Silence and Other Poems, Sarton, 1953.
LoT	Leaves of the Tree, Sarton, 1950.
L&R	The Lion and the Rose, Sarton, 1948.
PM	A Private Mythology, Sarton, 1966.

PARTIAL CHECKLIST OF INDIVIDUAL POEMS

ABSENCE OR PRESENCE
Virginia Quarterly Review. 42 (Summer, 1966), 403.

THE ACTION OF THE BEAUTIFUL
Voices. 154 (May-August, 1954), 25.

THE ACTION OF THERAPY see LETTERS TO A PSYCHIATRIST

ADDRESS TO THE HEART
IL. p. 31.
CP. p. 35.

ADVICE
EiA. p. 57.

AFTER A NIGHT OF RAIN THE BRILLIANT SCREEN/ (From the sequence entitled "Autumn Sonnets")
DF. p. 44.
CP. pp. 386-387.

AFTER A SHOCK
Virginia Quarterly Review. 42 (Summer, 1966), 409.

AFTER A TRAIN JOURNEY
L&R. p. 44.
CSSV. p. 34.
The Poetry of Railways. ed., K. Hopkins, London: L. Frewin, 1966, p. 103.
CP. p. 67.
To Be Alone. ed., Joan Victor, New York: Crown Pub., 1974, p. 38.

AFTER AN ISLAND
DF. p. 37.
CP. p. 381.

AFTER ANGER
The Malahet Review, April, 1968, pp. 54-55.

AFTER FOUR YEARS
New York Herald Tribune, February 26, 1956, p. 4.
Atlantic Monthly. 197 (March, 1956), 53.
Best Poems of 1956. Stanford: Stanford University Press, 1957, p. 79.
ITLA. p. 39.
CSSV. p. 100.
Harvard Poetry Reading (D 868.1/9), October 10, 1962.
The Various Light. eds., Leah Bodine Drake & Charles Arthur Muses, Switzerland: Aurora Press, 1964, p. 303.

AFTER SILENCE
IL. p. 36.
CP. p. 37.

AFTER THE TIGER
GoMS. p. 24.
CP. p. 321.

AFTERNOON ON WASHINGTON STREET
IL. p. 53.
Harvard Poetry Reading (D 13.3/2,3,4), August 6, 1941.
Harvard Poetry Reading (T 830.9/2), March 26, 1951.
CP. p. 40.

ALL DAY I WAS WITH TREES
DF. p. 32.
CP. p. 377.

ALL JOYS ARE SHARPER NOW I AM IN PAIN/
L&R. pp. 73-74.

ALL SOULS
Harper's Magazine. 215 (November, 1957), 49.
ITLA. p. 56.
CSSV. p. 105.
CP. p. 185.

ALONE I MAY BE, BUT STILL TWICE AWARE/
IL. p. 20.

ALONE ONE IS NEVER LONELY: THE SPIRIT ADVENTURES, WAKING/
(From the sequence entitled "Canticles")

IL. p. 43.

AMERICAN NOTEBOOK (includes the following poems:)
Where the grasses (Eastern Kansas)
Poetry. 59 (February, 1952), 235-237.
Boulder Dam
Poetry. 59 (February, 1942), 237-239.
L&R. p. 22.
CP. p. 51.
Ohio Country
Poetry. 59 (February, 1942), 239-240.
A Northerner Sees the Cottonfields for the First Time
Poetry. 59 (February, 1942), 240-241.
Of the Seasons
Poetry. 59 (February, 1942), 241-242.
L&R. p. 24.
CP. p. 53.

THE ANGELS AND THE FURIES
DF. p. 34.
Contempora. 2 (September/February, 1972), 17.
CP. p. 379.

THE ANNEALING
ADNH. P. 21.

ANNUNCIATION
Cornhill Magazine. 169 (Summer, 1957), 263-264.
ITLA. p. 52.
CSSV. p. 47.
CP. p. 184.

ANNUNCIATION
GoMS. p. 61.
CP. p. 347.

ANOTHER ISLAND
PM. p. 54.
CP. p. 256.

ANTELOPE
Poetry. 43 (October, 1933), 27.
EiA. p. 67 (poem appears with no title).

APOLOGY
EiA. p. 56.

APPLE TREE IN MAY
ADNH. p. 29.
CP. p. 306.

THE APPROACH--CALCUTTA
PM. p. 37.
CP. p. 243.

ARCHITECTURAL IMAGE
IL. p. 5.
Harvard Poetry Reading (D 13.3/2,3,4).
CP. p. 32.

AN ARTESIAN WELL
PM. p. 74.
CP. p. 274.

AS DOES NEW HAMPSHIRE
New York Herald Tribune, May 12, 1952, p. 14.
LoS. p. 8.
ADNH. p. 11.
CP. p. 118.

AS IF THE HOUSE WERE DYING OR ALREADY DEAD/
(From the sequence entitled "Autumn Sonnets")
DF. p. 45.
CP. p. 387.

AS MUSIC IN A STILL HOUSE OUT OF SILENCE SPRINGS/
IL. p. 39.

AT CHARTRES
Massachusetts Review. 1 (Summer, 1960), 719.
GoMS. p. 62.
CP. p. 348.

AT DELPHI
PM. p. 57.
CP. p. 258.

AT LINDOS
Beloit Poetry Journal. 15 (Fall, 1964), 4-9.
Best Poems of 1964. Palo Alto: Pacific Books, 1965, p. 108.
PM. p. 55.
The Women Poets in English. ed., Ann Stanford, New York: Herder & Herder, 1973, p. 357.
CP. p. 257.

AT MUZOT
Colorado Quarterly. 4 (Spring, 1956), 354.
ITLA. p. 37.
Archive of Recorded Poetry and Literature. Washington, D. C.: U. S. Library of Congress, 1961.
CSSV. p. 63.
Harvard Poetry Reading (D 868.1/9) October 10, 1962.
CP. p. 176.

AT THE BOTTOM OF THE GREEN FIELD
LoS. p. 5.
Archive of Recorded Poetry and Literature. Washington, D. C.: U. S. Library of Congress, 1961.
CSSV. p. 61.

AUGENBLICK
LoS. p. 48.
ADNH. p. 54.

AUTUMN AGAIN
DF. p. 56.

AUTUMN: ANNISQUAM
LoT. p. 17.

AUTUMN SONNET
Falling Fountains. 1 (January, 1974), 15.

THE AUTUMN SONNETS (includes the following sonnets:)
Under the leaves an infant love lies dead/
DF. p. 43.
CP. p. 385.
If I can let you go as trees let go/
DF. p. 43.
CP. p. 385.
I wake to gentle mist over the meadow/
DF. pp. 43-44.
CP. pp. 385-386.
I never thought that it could be, not once/
DF. p. 44.
CP. p. 386.
After a night of rain the brilliant screen/
DF. p. 44.
CP. pp. 386-387.
As if the house were dying or already dead/
DF. p. 45.
CP. p. 387.

Twice I have set my heart upon a sharing/
DF. p. 45.
CP. p. 387.
I ponder it again and know for sure/
DF. p. 45.
CP. p. 387-388.
This was our testing year after the first/
DF. p. 46.
CP. p. 388.
We watched the waterfalls, rich and baroque/
DF. p. 46.
CP. p. 388-389.
For steadfast flame wood must be seasoned/
DF. p. 47.
CP. p. 389.

THE BALLAD OF JOHNNY
GoMS. p. 16.

THE BALLAD OF RUBY
GoMS. p. 14.
Pictures that Storm Inside My Head. ed., Richard Peck, New York: Avon Books, 1976.

BALLAD OF THE SIXTIES
GoMS. p. 11.
CP. p. 313.

BALLADS OF THE TRAVELER
Beloit Poetry Journal. 15 (Fall, 1964), 4-9.
PM. p. 60.
CP. p. 260.

BAROQUE IMAGE (FOR ANY ARTIST)
Outposts. 63 (Winter, 1964), 19.
Voices. 2 (1965), 25.
PM. p. 107.
CP. p. 299.

BEARS AND WATERFALLS
Ante. 3 (Summer, 1967), 60-61.
GoMS. p. 47.
CP. p. 339.

THE BEAUTIFUL PAUSES
PM. p. 13.
CP. p. 223.

BECAUSE THIS STRANGE ADVENTURE IS SO GRAVE/
IL. p. 21.

BECAUSE WHAT I WANT MOST IS PERMANENCE
LoS. p. 54.
CP. p. 137.

THE BEECH WOOD
Ladies Home Journal. 72 (October, 1955), 100.

BEHIND WHAT LITTLE MIRROR LIES THE COUNTRY OF YOUR VOICE?/
IL. p. 38.

BERCEUSE
EiA. p. 55.

BEYOND THE QUESTION
GoMS. p. 69.
CP. p. 355.

BINDING THE DRAGON
The Nation. 183 (November 10, 1956), 410.
ITLA. p. 61.
CSSV. p. 87.
Harvard Poetry Reading (D 868.1/9) October 10, 1962.
CP. p. 187.

BIRD OF GLASS
Atlantic Monthly. 166 (September, 1940), 364.

THE BIRTHDAY
L&R. p. 100.
CP. p. 96.

BIRTHDAY ON THE ACROPOLIS
PM. p. 47.
CP. p. 251.

BIRTHDAY PRESENT
DF. p. 65.
CP. p. 398.

BOULDER DAM
(From the sequence entitled "American Notebook")
Poetry. 59 (February, 1942), 237-239.
L&R. p. 22.
CP. p. 51.

BOY BY THE WATERFALL
LoT. p. 32.
LoS. p. 89.
CSSV. p. 64.
CP. p. 109.

A BUNCH OF ROSES
Voices. 151 (May-August, 1953), 24.

BURIAL
DF. p. 61.
CP. p. 394.

BUT PARTING IS RETURN, THE COMING HOME/
(From the sequence entitled "These Images Remain")
Atlantic Monthly. 183 (March, 1949), 58-59.
LoS. p. 74.
CP. p. 145.

BUT TOUCH IS MEANS AND SIGNIFIES NO MORE/
IL. p. 17.

BY MOONLIGHT
Modern Love Poems. ed., D. J. Klemer, New York: Doubleday & Co., 1961, p. 78.
ITLA. p. 69.
CP. p. 196.

THE CAGED BIRD
LoS. p. 32.
CP. p. 130.

CANTICLES (includes the following poems:)
IL. pp. 38-50.
Behind what little mirror lies the country of your voice?/ p. 38.
As music in a still house out of silence springs/ p. 39.
Passion like radium is luminous in essence/ p. 40.
The wind which swept the earth has mounted the trees/ p. 41.
If there is mercy it is not, no, not in the wind/ p. 42.
Alone one is never lonely: the spirit adventures waking/ p. 43.
To stand on the earth again is a grave event/ p. 44.
That night we went outside the gate beyond the wood/ p. 45.

There are voices in the garden. Day folds itself into/ p. 46.
The spirit comes back to silence like a dove/ p. 47.
We sat smoking at a table by the river/ p. 48.
Is it a flower pressed or a perfect leaf/ p. 50.
Harvard Poetry Reading (D 13.3/2,3,4) August 6, 1941.
Now it is evening coming and you are not here/ p. 49.

A CELEBRATION (FOR GEORGE SARTON)
New Poems By American Poets #2. ed., Rolfe Humphries, New York: Ballantine Books, 1957, pp. 136-137.
Isis. 48 (September, 1957), 285.
ITLA. p. 9.
Archive of Recorded Poetry and Literature. Washington, D.C.: U.S. Library of Congress, 1961.
CSSV. p. 103.
Harvard Poetry Reading (D 868.1/9) October 10, 1962.
When Women Look at Men. ed., John Kouwenhoven and Janice Thaddeus, New York: Harper & Row, 1963, p. 240.

CELEBRATIONS
University Review (University of Kansas City). 60 (Winter, 1942), 88-89.
The Best Poems of 1943. ed., Thomas Moult, New York: Harcourt, Brace, 1944, pp. 69-71.
L&R. p. 101.

CEREMONY see CEREMONY CORN DANCE, SAN FELIPE

CEREMONY CORN DANCE, SAN FELIPE
Colorado Quarterly. 4 (Spring, 1956), 355-356.
ITLA. pp. 54-55. (Under the title "Ceremony")

CHARLESTON PLANTATIONS
Atlantic Monthly. 167 (April, 1941), 487.
Anthology of Magazine Verse and Yearbook of American Poetry for 1938-1941. ed., Alan F. Pater, New York: The Paebar Company, 1942, p. 412.
L&R. p. 17.
CSSV. p. 27.
CP. p. 48.

A CHILD'S JAPAN
Colorado Quarterly. 14 (Spring, 1966), 307.
PM. p. 17.
CP. p. 224.

A CHINESE LANDSCAPE
Yankee, September, 1972, p. 208.
DF. p. 25.
CP. p. 372.

A CHRISTMAS ELEGY
Yankee, December, 1968, p. 196.

CHRISTMAS LETTER TO A PSYCHIATRIST: FOR MARYNIA FARNHAM
(From the series entitled LETTERS TO A PSYCHIATRIST
Contempora. 2 (September/February, 1972), 24.
DF. pp. 69-71.
CP. pp. 400-402.

CHRISTMAS, 1974
New York Times, December 24, 1974, p. 19.

CHRISTMAS TREE
ADNH. p. 19.

THE CLAVICHORD
Harvard Poetry Reading (T 851.1/1) n.d.
L&R. p. 47.
Untune the Sky. comp., Helen Plotz, New York: Thomas Y. Crowell, 1957, p. 18.
CP. p. 69.

COLD NIGHT
Virginia Quarterly Review. 42 (Summer, 1966), 403-404.

COLD SPRING
University Review. (University of Kansas City) 8 (March 3, 1941), 176.

COLORADO MOUNTAIN
Harvard Poetry Reading (D 13.3/2,3,4) August 6, 1941.
Briarcliff Quarterly. 2 (April 5, 1945), 6.
L&R. p. 23.
CP. p. 52.

COMPOSITION
DF. p. 55.
CP. p. 393.

CONSIDERATIONS
IL. p. 57.

CONSTRAINED IT CAN BE. SHORT OF DEATH/
(From the sequence entitled "Over Troubled Water")
Francis Marion Review. 1 (1975), 14.

THE CONTEMPLATION OF WISDOM see LETTERS TO A PSYCHIATRIST

THE CONTEST
Ante. 3 (Summer, 1967), 62.

CONVERSATIONS IN BLACK AND WHITE
The Nation. 187 (November 1, 1958), 305.
The Golden Year. eds., Melville Crane, et al., New York: Books for Libraries Press, 1960, p. 239.
PM. p. 99.
CP. p. 291.

CONVERSATIONS ON THE TELEPHONE
Saturday Review of Literature. 14 (September 5, 1936), 12.
IL. p. 29.

A COUNTRY HOUSE (FOR SHIO SAKANISHI)
Colorado Quarterly. 14 (Spring, 1966), 309.
PM. p. 19.
CP. p. 226.

A COUNTRY INCIDENT
Poetry. 99 (November, 1961), 98.
PM. p. 77.
ADNH. p. 51.
CP. p. 277.

A COUNTRY OF SILENCE
DF. p. 36.

DEAR SOLID EARTH
DF. p. 18.
CP. p. 366.

DEATH AND THE LOVERS
ITLA. p. 72.
CSSV. p. 78.
Harvard Poetry Reading (D 868.1/9) October 10, 1962.
CP. p. 198.

DEATH AND THE TURTLE
PM. p. 91.

CP. p. 286.

DEATH OF A PSYCHIATRIST
Beloit Poetry Journal. 15 (Fall, 1964), 4-9.
PM. p. 97.
CP. p. 289.

DEFEAT: HERE WHERE WE NEED NOT MOVE NOR SPEAK/
IL. p. 24.

DEFINITION
Life and Letters Today. 29 (May, 1941), 152.
L&R. p. 41.

DEFINITION
Harvard Poetry Reading (D 13.3/2,3,4) August 6, 1941.
ITLA. p. 65.
Modern Love Poems. ed., D. J. Klemer, New York: Doubleday, 1961, p. 74.
A Time to Love. ed., Joan Berg Victor, New York: Crown Publishers, 1971, p. 79.
CP. p. 190.

DEFINITION OF LOVE
L&R. p. 68.

DENY THE PASSION THAT IS BOUND IN YOU/
IL. p. 22.

DER ABSCHIED
Kenyon Review. 23 (Spring, 1961), 275-276.
CSSV. p. 143.
Harvard Poetry Reading (D 868.1/9) October 10, 1962.
CP. p. 218.

DIALOGUE
New Yorker. 29 (April 18, 1953), 134.
ITLA. p. 16.
Shady Hill News, February, 1959, p. 3.
CP. p. 161.

DIFFICULT SCENE
(From the sequence entitled "Theme and Variation: Santa Fe, New Mexico")
Poetry. 68 (May, 1946), 76-77.
L&R. p. 5.
CP. p. 55.

DIRGE
<u>LoT</u>. p. 33.

DIVORCE OF LOVERS (includes the following sonnets:)
Now these two warring halves are to be parted/
<u>Cornhill Magazine</u>. 171 (Autumn, 1960), 459.
<u>CSSV</u>. p. 125.
<u>CP</u>. p. 201.
I shall not see the end of this unweaving/
<u>Cornhill Magazine</u>. 171 (Autumn, 1960), 459.
<u>CSSV</u>. p. 125.
<u>CP</u>. p. 201.
One death's true death, and that is--not to care/
<u>Cornhill Magazine</u>. 171 (Autumn, 1960), 460.
<u>CSSV</u>. p. 126.
<u>CP</u>. p. 201.
Did you achieve this with a simple word/
<u>Cornhill Magazine</u>. 171 (Autumn, 1960), 460.
<u>CSSV</u>. p. 126.
<u>CP</u>. p. 202.
What price serenity these cruel days/
<u>Cornhill Magazine</u>. 171 (Autumn, 1960), 461.
<u>CSSV</u>. p. 127.
<u>CP</u>. p. 202.
Dear fellow-sufferer, dear cruelty/
<u>Cornhill Magazine</u>. 171 (Autumn, 1960), 461.
<u>CSSV</u>. p. 127.
<u>CP</u>. p. 202.
Your greatness withers when it shuts out grief/
<u>Cornhill Magazine</u>. 171 (Autumn, 1960), 462.
<u>CSSV</u>. p. 128.
<u>CP</u>. p. 203.
Now we have lost the heartways and the word/
<u>Cornhill Magazine</u>. 171 (Autumn, 1960), 463.
<u>CSSV</u>. p. 128.
<u>CP</u>. p. 203.
What if a homing pigeon lost its home/
<u>Cornhill Magazine</u>. 171 (Autumn), 1960, 463.
<u>CSSV</u>. p. 129.
<u>CP</u>. p. 204.
So drive back hating Love and loving Hate/
<u>Cornhill Magazine</u>. 171 (Autumn, 1960), 464.
<u>CSSV</u>. p. 130.
<u>CP</u>. p. 205.
It does not mean that we shall find the place/
<u>Cornhill Magazine</u>. 171 (Autumn, 1960), 464.
<u>CSSV</u>. p. 130.
<u>CP</u>. p. 205.

Others have cherished, perhaps loved me more/
Cornhill Magazine. 171 (Autumn, 1960), 464.
CSSV. p. 130.
CP. p. 205.
Wild seas, wild seas, and the gulls veering close/
Cornhill Magazine. 171 (Autumn, 1960), 465.
CSSV. p. 131.
CP. p. 206.
For all the loving words and difficult/
Cornhill Magazine. 171 (Autumn, 1960), 465.
CSSV. p. 131.
CP. p. 206.
As I look out on the long swell of fields/
Cornhill Magazine. 171 (Autumn, 1960), 466.
CSSV. p. 132.
CP. p. 206.
The cat sleeps on my desk in the pale sun/
Cornhill Magazine. 171 (Autumn, 1960), 466.
CSSV. p. 132.
CP. p. 207.
After a night of driving rain, the skies/
Cornhill Magazine. 171 (Autumn, 1960), 467.
CSSV. p. 133.
CP. p. 207.
These riches burst from every barren tree/
Cornhill Magazine. 171 (Autumn, 1960), 467.
CSSV. p. 133.
CP. p. 208.
Where do I go? Nowhere. And who am I?/
Cornhill Magazine. 171 (Autumn, 1960), 468.
CSSV. p. 134.
CP. p. 208.
Now silence, silence, silence, and within it/
Cornhill Magazine. 171 (Autumn, 1960), 468.
CSSV. p. 134.
CP. p. 208.

DON'T TOUCH ME. I WOULD KEEP US STILL APART/
EiA. p. 68.

THE DOUBTS MOVE INWARD AS THE CIRCLE NARROWS/
L&R. p. 74.

THE DREAM
Botteghe Oscure. 9 (1952), 295-296.
LoS. p. 37.

DRY SUMMER
ADNH. p. 38.

DUTCH INTERIOR: PIETER DE HOOCH (1629-1682)
Contempora. 1 (October /November, 1970), 32.
GoMS. p. 43.
CP. p. 338.

THE DYING
Harvard Poetry Reading (T 830.9/2) March 26, 1951.

THE EARTH IS SLIM BETWEEN TWO WHO HAVE SEEN/
EiA. p. 79.

EASTER EGG
Saturday Review of Literature. 38 (April 9, 1955), 31.

EASTER MORNING
Virginia Quarterly Review. 42 (Summer, 1966), 405.
GoMS. p. 65.
CP. p. 351.

EASTER, 1968
GoMS. p. 18.

EASTER, 1971 see LETTERS TO A PSYCHIATRIST

EINE KLEINE SNAILMUSIK
New Yorker. 22 (January 25, 1947), 38.
GoMS. p. 51.
CP. p. 343.

ELEGY FOR A BLACK CAT
A Celebration of Cats. ed., Jean Burden, New York: Paul Eriksson, Inc., 1974, pp. 73-74.

ELEGY FOR KATHLEEN FERRIER
Pennsylvania Literary Review. 8 (1957), 9.

ELEGY FOR LOUISE BOGAN
DF. p. 66.
CP. p. 399.

ELEGY (FOR META BUDRY TURIAN)
Cornhill Magazine, Autumn, 1961, pp. 236-237.
PM. p. 95.
CP. p. 287.

AN ELEGY (THE POET LEAVES THE ACADEMY)
Virginia Quarterly Review. 42 (Summer, 1966), 406-407.

ENCOUNTER IN APRIL (includes the following sonnets:)
EiA. pp. 7-9.
We came together softly like two deer/ p. 7.
'No spring can be eternal, nor can this'/ p. 7.
If I have poured myself with reserve/ p. 8.
For you a leopard-word--no deer, no pheasant/ p. 8.
Not without grace and certainly with pride/ p. 9.

EPIPHANY
Massachusetts Review. 1 (Summer, 1960), 719.

EVEN SUCH FERVOR MUST SEEK OUT AN END/
(From the sequence entitled "These Images Remain")
LoS. p. 69.
Modern Love Poems. ed., D. J. Klemer, New York: Doubleday, 1961, p. 31.
CP. p. 144.

EVENING IN FRANCE
CSSV. p. 35.
CP. p. 123.

EVENING JOURNEY
Atlantic Monthly. 191 (March, 1953), 50.

EVENING MEAL
LoT. p. 27.

EVENING MUSIC
Saturday Review of Literature. 33 (August 19, 1950), 7.
LoT. p. 25.
LoS. p. 63.
CSSV. p. 50.
CP. p. 106.

EVENING WALK IN FRANCE
The Lyric. 46 (Fall, 1966), 80.
GoMS. p. 42.
CP. p. 337.

EVERYWHERE, IN MY GARDEN, IN MY THOUGHT/
(From the sequence entitled "Over Troubled Water")
Francis Marion Review. 1 (1975), 11.

AN EXCHANGE OF GIFTS
PM. p. 30.
CP. p. 238.

THE FALL see THESE WERE HER NIGHTLY JOURNEYS

THE FALL
Colorado Quarterly. 4 (Spring, 1956), 353-354.
ITLA. p. 63.
CSSV. p. 73.
CP. p. 188.

FALL OF PETALS
EiA. p. 58.

FAUN'S DEATH
EiA. p. 59.

THE FEAR OF ANGELS see LETTERS TO A PSYCHIATRIST

FEBRUARY DAYS
DF. p. 51.
CP. p. 390.

FEBRUARY OWLS
Plume and Sword. 4 (May 4, 1964), 14.

A FIELD OF GRAIN
Voices. 169 (May/August, 1959), 7-8.
Best Poems of 1959. Palo Alto: Pacific Books, 1961, p. 88.

THE FIG
Yankee. 30 (June, 1966), 168.
GoMS. p. 52.
CP. p. 343.

THE FIRST AUTUMN
LoS. p. 2.
CSSV. p. 99.
CP. p. 115.

FIRST LOVE
(From the sequence entitled "Words on the Wind")
Poetry. 37 (December, 1930), 144.

FIRST SNOW
EiA. p. 1.
CP. p. 19.

A FLOWER-ARRANGING SUMMER
The Lyric. 41 (Summer, 1961), 62-63.
CSSV. p. 140.
ADNH. p. 31.
CP. p. 215.

FOR A TEACHER OF MATHEMATICS: RUTH EDGETT
LoT. p. 31.
Shady Hill News, February, 1959, p. 2.

FOR ELEONORA DUSE
EiA. p. 40.

FOR KEATS AND MOZART
EiA. p. 64.

FOR MARIETTE LYDIS
EiA. p. 34.

FOR ROSALINE (ON HER SEVENTY-FIFTH BIRTHDAY)
GoMS. p. 39.
CP. p. 333.

FOR STEADFAST FLAME WOOD MUST BE SEASONED/
(From the sequence entitled "The Autumn Sonnets")
DF. p. 47.
CP. p. 389.

FOR YOU A LEOPARD-WORD--NO DEER, NO PHEASANT/
(From the sequence entitled "Encounter in April")
Poetry. 40 (April, 1932), 15.
EiA. p. 8.

FOR YOU WHO SHOULD HAVE STOOD BESIDE ME HERE/
IL. p. 19.

FORE THOUGHT
ITLA. p. 65.
Modern Love Poems. ed., D. J. Klemer, New York: Doubleday, 1961, p. 89.
CP. p. 191 (variant spelling of title, "Forethought").

FORETHOUGHT see FORE THOUGHT

THE FOUNTAIN
Voices. 178 (May-August, 1962), 28-29.

FRANZ A GOOSE
Cornhill Magazine. 171 (Winter, 1959-1960), 101-103.
Atlantic Monthly. 205 (May, 1960), 52.
Best Poems of 1960. Palo Alto: Pacific Books, 1962, p. 105.
Harvard Poetry Reading (D 868.1/9) October 10, 1962.
PM. p. 85.
CP. p. 285.

FRIENDSHIP: THE STORMS
GoMS. p. 41.
CP. p. 335.

FROG, THAT NAKED CREATURE
Hudson Review. 9 (Spring, 1956), 44-45.
ITLA. p. 42.
Archive of Recorded Poetry and Literature. Washington, D.C.: U. S. Library of Congress, 1961.
CSSV. p. 88.
Harvard Poetry Reading (D 868.1/9) October 10, 1962.

FROGS AND PHOTOGRAPHERS
Yankee. 30 (August, 1966), 148.
GoMS. p. 50.

FROM A TRAIN WINDOW
IL. p. 55.

FROM ALL OUR JOURNEYS
LoS. p. 22.
CSSV. p. 43.
CP. p. 124.

FROM CORNWALL
EiA. p. 26.

FROM MEN WHO DIED DELUDED
Saturday Review of Literature. 16 (May 29, 1937), 4.
IL. p. 52.
Harvard Poetry Reading (D 13.3/2,3,4) August 6, 1941.
New Treasury of War Poetry. ed., Herbert Clarke, New York: Houghton Mifflin Co., 1943, p. 131.
CP. p. 39.

FRUIT OF LONELINESS
(From the sequence entitled "Words on the Wind")
Poetry. 37 (December, 1930), 146.

A FUGUE OF WINGS
The Lyric. 45 (Winter, 1965), 12-13.
PM. p. 69.
ADNH. p. 14.
CP. p. 269.

FULFILLMENT
DF. p. 40.
CP. p. 384.

THE FULLNESS OF TIME
Botteghe Oscure. 9 (1952), 294-295.
LoS. p. 86.

THE FURIES
Audience. 5 (Summer, 1958), 40-41.
Archive of Recorded Poetry and Literature. Washington, D.C.: U.S. Library of Congress, 1961.
CSSV. p. 86.
Harvard Poetry Reading (D 868.1/9) October 10, 1962.
CP. p. 162.

THE GARDEN OF CHILDHOOD
The Lyric. 46 (Fall, 1966), 82.
DF. p. 54.

GESTALT AT SIXTY
The Cornhill Magazine, Autumn, 1972, pp. 316-319.
DF. p. 11.
CP. p. 361.

THE GHOST
Pennsylvania Literary Review. 5 (1954), 17.

THE GHOST IN THE MACHINE
Transatlantic Review. 19 (Autumn, 1965), 71-72.

GIANT IN THE GARDEN
LoS. p. 83.
CP. p. 150.

THE GIFT
New York Herald Tribune, November 21, 1952, p. 18.

THE GIFTS
Briarcliff Quarterly. 3 (April, 1946), 62-63.

GIRL WITH 'CELLO
GoMS. p. 36.
CP. p. 332.
Pictures that Storm Inside My Head. ed., Richard Peck, New York: Avon Books, 1976.

GLASS OF WATER
Cornhill Magazine. 174 (Winter, 1964-1965), 293-294.
ADNH. p. 37.
CP. p. 307.

THE GODHEAD AS LYNX
GoMS. p. 66.
CP. p. 352.

GRANTED THIS WORLD
IL. p. 10.
CSSV. p. 48.

THE GREAT CATS AND THE BEARS
Literary Review. 7 (Summer, 1964), 512-513.
A Celebration of Cats. ed., Jean Burden, New York: Paul Eriksson, 1974, pp. 154-155.

THE GREAT PLAIN OF INDIA SEEN FROM THE AIR
Texas Quarterly. 4 (Winter, 1964), 143-144.
PM. p. 43.

THE GREAT SNOW
LoT. p. 18.

THE GREAT TRANSPARENCIES
GoMS. p. 40.
Cornhill Magazine, Spring, 1972, p. 187.
CP. p. 334.

A GREEK MEAL
PM. p. 51.

GREEN SONG
New Yorker. 32 (August 11, 1956), 59.
ITLA. p. 31.
Archive of Recorded Poetry and Literature. Washington, D.C.: U.S. Library of Congress, 1961.
CP. p. 170

GREETING
IL. p. 62.

A GUEST
Yankee. 31 (July, 1967), 180.
ADNH. p. 53.
CP. p. 309.

HANDS
EiA. p. 53.

A HARD DEATH
GoMS. p. 57.
CP. p. 344.

HARVEST
Yale Review. 35 (September, 1945), 29.
L&R. p. 68.

HAWAIIAN PALM
GoMS. p. 53.

HERE ARE THE PEACEFUL DAYS WE NEVER KNEW/ (From the sequence entitled "These Images Remain")
Atlantic Monthly. 183 (March, 1949), 58.
LoS. p. 78.
CP. p. 147.

HERE LET ME LIE QUIET UPON YOUR SHOULDER/ (From the sequence entitled "These Images Remain")
Atlantic Monthly. 183 (March, 1949), 59.

HEUREUX QUI, COMME ULYSSE ...
PM. p. 65.
ADNH. p. 56 (under title "Plant Dreaming Deep")
CP. p. 265.

HOMAGE TO FLANDERS
Poetry. 65 (February, 1945), 233-234.
L&R. p. 83.
Archive of Recorded Poetry and Literature. Washington, D. C.: U. S. Library of Congress, 1961.
CSSV. p. 31.
Harvard Poetry Reading (D 868.1/9) October 10, 1962.
CP. p. 85.

THE HORSE-PULLING
PM. p. 85.

ADNH. p. 40.
CP. p. 282.

HOUR OF PROOF
CSSV. p. 142.
ADNH. p. 44.
CP. p. 217.

THE HOUSE IN WINTER
New Yorker. 39 (January 4, 1964), 65.
Best Poems of 1964. Palo Alto: Pacific Books, 1965, p. 110.
PM. p. 67.
ADNH. p. 14.
CP. p. 267.

HUMPTY DUMPTY
Poetry. 74 (August, 1949), 273.
LoS. p. 82.
CSSV. p. 85.
CP. p. 149.

I HAD NOT DREAMED THIS TOUCH WOULD TURN TO STONE/
IL. p. 16.

I HAVE BEEN NOURISHED BY THIS LONELINESS/
EiA. p. 80.

I HAVE WATCHED TIME FALLING ACROSS YOUR HAIR/
(From the sequence entitled "Portraits of Three Women")
EiA. p. 38.

I NEVER THOUGHT THAT IT COULD BE, NOT ONCE/
(From the sequence entitled "The Autumn Sonnets")
DF. p. 44.
CP. p. 386.

I PICKED LOVE FROM THE BOUGH ON WHICH IT SWINGS/
EiA. p. 72.

I PONDER IT AGAIN AND KNOW FOR SURE/
(From the sequence entitled "The Autumn Sonnets")
DF. p. 45.
CP. p. 387-388.

I SIT AT MY DESK IN A HUGE SILENCE/
(From the sequence entitled "Over Troubled Water")
Francis Marion Review. 1 (1975), 11.

I SPEAK OF CHANGE see LETTERS TO A PSYCHIATRIST

I WAKE TO GENTLE MIST OVER THE MEADOW/
(From the sequence entitled "The Autumn Sonnets")
DF. p. 43.
CP. pp. 385-386.

I WENT BEYOND THE EARTH AND STOOD OUTSIDE/
EiA. p. 76.

IF I CAN LET YOU GO AS TREES LET GO/
(From the sequence entitled "The Autumn Sonnets")
DF. p. 43.
CP. p. 385.

IF I COULD LAY MY HEAD WITHIN THE SCOPE/
EiA. p. 78.

IF I HAVE POURED MYSELF WITHOUT RESERVE/
(From the sequence entitled "Encounter in April")
EiA. p. 8.

IF I SIT SMOULDERING NOW AS EARLY WHEAT/
EiA. p. 70.

IF THERE IS MERCY IT IS NOT, NOT IN THE WIND/
(From the sequence entitled "Canticles")
IL. p. 42.

IF YOU TAKE REFUGE IN A WORD THEN BEAR/
(From the sequence entitled "Over Troubled Water")
Francis Marion Review. 1 (1975), 15.

ILLUMINATION EXISTS see LETTERS TO A PSYCHIATRIST; I SPEAK OF CHANGE

IMAGE
London Mercury. 36 (September, 1937), 419.

THE IMAGES
LoT. p. 36.

IN A DRY LAND
LoS. p. 60.
CSSV. p. 72.
CP. p. 140.

IN DEEP CONCERN
Atlantic Monthly. 169 (May, 1942), 573.
L&R. p. 16.

IN KASHMIR
PM. p. 45.
CP. p. 249.

IN MEMORIAM
University Review. (University of Kansas City) 12 (Spring, 1946), 212-213.
L&R. p. 51.
Harvard Poetry Reading (T 830.9/2) March 26, 1951, (excerpt)
CP. p. 71.

IN TEXAS
Atlantic Monthly. 167 (April, 1941), 485.
Harvard Poetry Reading (D 13.3/2,3,4) August 6, 1941.
Anthology of Magazine Verse and Yearbook of American Poetry for 1938-1941. ed., Alan F. Pater, New York: The Paebar Company, 1942, p. 413.
L&R. p. 20.
America in Verse: A Treasury of Patriotic Poetry. comp., Donald T. Kauffman, New York: Pyramid Books, 1968, pp. 77-78.

IN THAT DEEP WOOD
L&R. p. 50.

IN THE INN AT KYOTO
Colorado Quarterly. 14 (Spring, 1966), 311-312.
PM. p. 28.
CP. p. 234.

IN TIME LIKE AIR
New Yorker. 32 (May 12, 1956), 42.
ITLA. p. 49.
Modern Love Poems. ed., D. J. Klemer, New York: Doubleday, 1961, p. 34.
CSSV. p. 82.
The New Yorker Book of Poems. New York: Viking Press, 1969, p. 343.
CP. p. 182.

INDIAN DANCES
L&R. p. 26.
CP. p. 58.

INNER SPACE

Red Clay Reader. 7 (1970), 72.
DF. p. 20.
CP. p. 368.

INNUMERABLE FRIEND

Saturday Review of Literature. 32 (March 19, 1949), 20.
LoS. p. 27.
A Way of Knowing. ed., Gerald D. McDonald, New York: Thomas Y. Crowell, 1959, pp. 186-187.
CSSV. p. 119.
CP. p. 128.

INTERVIEW

EiA. p. 54.

AN INTRUDER

GoMS. p. 37.

INVOCATION

IL. p. 4.
Saturday Review of Literature. 38 (March 12, 1955), 18.
GoMS. p. 72.
CP. p. 358.

THE INVOCATION TO KALI

GoMS. pp. 19-23.
Poetry. 117 (February, 1971), 314-321.
Rising Tides: Twentieth Century American Women Poets. eds., Laura Chester & Sharon Barba, New York: Washington Square Press, 1973, pp. 64-67. (Only sections I, II, V)
CP. pp. 316-320.

IS IT A FLOWER PRESSED OR A PERFECT LEAF/
(From the sequence entitled "Canticles")

IL. p. 50.

IS THIS HEART, EMPEROR, SETTING AT YOUR FEET/

IL. p. 14.

IS YOUR HEART STIFF AND SORE PARTED FROM ME/

L&R. p. 73.

ISLANDS AND WELLS

LoT. p. 28.
CP. p. 108.

ITALIAN GARDEN
New Yorker. 29 (August 1, 1953), 53.
LoS. p. 92.
Archive of Recorded Poetry and Literature. Washington, D. C.: U. S. Library of Congress, 1961.
CSSV. p. 39.
CP. p. 152.

ITALIAN VERSE
New Yorker. 29 (August 1, 1953), 53.

IT'S THE TIME OF BREAKING, YOUR HOUSE SOLD/
(From the sequence entitled "Over Troubled Water")
Francis Marion Review. 1 (1975), 16.

JAPANESE PRINTS (includes the following poems:)
Four Views of Fujiyama
PM. p. 22.
CP. p. 229.
On the Way to Lake Chuzen-ji
Northeast, 1964, p. 11.
Cornhill Magazine, Summer, 1966, p. 293.
PM. p. 22.
CP. p. 229.
Lake Chuzen-ji
PM. p. 22.
CP. p. 229.
Enkaku-ji, Zen Monastery
PM. p. 23.
CP. p. 230.
Three Variations on a Theme
Cornhill Magazine, Summer, 1966, p. 293.
PM. p. 23.
CP. p. 230.
Seen from a Train
Northeast, 1964, p. 11.
PM. p. 23.
CP. p. 230.
The Leopards at Nanzen-ji
Northeast, 1964, p. 11.
Cornhill Magazine, Summer, 1966, p. 294.
PM. p. 24.
CP. p. 231.
At Katsura, Imperial Village
Northeast, 1964, p. 11.
Cornhill Magazine, Summer, 1966, p. 294.
PM. p. 24.
CP. p. 231.

The Inland Sea
PM. p. 24.
CP. p. 232.
Tourist
PM. p. 25.
CP. p. 232.
In a Bus
Cornhill Magazine, Summer, 1966, p. 293.
PM. p. 25.
CP. p. 232.
Carp Garden
Cornhill Magazine, Summer, 1966, p. 294.
PM. p. 25.
CP. p. 232.

JONAH
Outposts. 64 (Spring, 1965), 15.
Virginia Quarterly Review. 42 (Summer, 1966), 406.
GoMS. p. 64.
CP. p. 350.

JOURNEY BY TRAIN
New Yorker. 28 (June 7, 1952), 30.
LoS. p. 16.
CP. p. 122.

JOURNEY TOWARD POETRY
Saturday Review of Literature. 36 (August 29, 1953), 12.
LoS. p. 91.
CP. p. 151.

JOY IN PROVENCE
PM. p. 105.
CP. p. 297.

JOY WILL NOT EVER FLOURISH AT YOUR NEED/
EiA. p. 73.

THE JUST EXCHANGES
The Husk. 29 (December, 1949), 49.

KEW
EiA. p. 29.

KINDS OF WIND
Atlantic Monthly. 192 (September, 1953), 33.
LoS. p. 64.

CP. p. 103.
New York Times Book Review, May 16, 1954, p. 2.

KOT'S HOUSE
LoT. p. 21.
CP. p. 103.

KYOKO
Colorado Quarterly. 14 (Spring, 1966), 310-314.
PM. p. 20.
CP. p. 227.

THE LADY AND THE UNICORN
Atlantic Monthly. 181 (January, 1948), 89.
L&R. p. 65.
Archive of Recorded Poetry and Literature. Washington, D.C.: U.S. Library of Congress, 1961.
CSSV. p. 51.
CP. p. 78.

LADY WITH A FALCON: FLEMISH TAPESTRY, 15TH CENTURY
ITLA. p. 26.

LAMENT
IL. p. 8.

LAMENT FOR TOBY, A FRENCH POODLE
New Yorker. 30 (October 16, 1954), 143.
ITLA. p. 28.
CP. p. 169.

THE LAND OF SILENCE
LoS. p. 34.
CSSV. p. 22.
CP. p. 131.

LANDSCAPE
IL. p. 6.

LANDSCAPE PURSUED BY A CLOUD
LoT. p. 24.
CP. p. 105.

LAST NIGHT I STOOD BESIDE YOU IN YOUR HELL/
(From the sequence entitled "Over Troubled Water")
Francis Marion Review. 1 (1975), 15.

A LAST WORD (FOR MY STUDENTS AT WELLESLEY COLLEGE)
GoMS. p. 34.
Cornhill Magazine, Spring, 1972, pp. 185-186.
CP. p. 331.

A LATE MOWING
PM. p. 76.
ADNH. p. 47.
CP. p. 276.

LAZARUS
PM. p. 63.
CP. p. 263.

LEARNING ABOUT WATER
PM. p. 72.
CP. p. 272.

LEAVES BEFORE THE WIND
New Poems by American Poets. ed., Rolfe Humphries, New York: Ballantine Books, 1953, p. 136.
Botteghe Oscure. 14 (1954), 273-276.
LoS. p. 58.
Modern Love Poems. ed., D. J. Klemer, New York: Doubleday, 1961, p. 21.
CSSV. p. 71.
CP. p. 139.

THE LEGEND HAUNTS US STILL. EACH OF US WEARS/
(From the sequence entitled "Over Troubled Water")
Francis Marion Review. 1 (1975), 14.

LET NO WIND COME
(From the sequence entitled "Words on the Wind")
Poetry. 37 (December, 1930), 145.

LETTER FROM CHICAGO
LoS. p. 93.
CP. p. 153.

LETTER TO AN INDIAN FRIEND
LoS. p. 35.
Harvard Poetry Reading (T 830.9/2) March 26, 1951.
CSSV. p. 23.
CP. p. 132.

LETTER TO JAMES STEPHENS
London Mercury. 38 (August, 1938), 305-306.
IL. p. 63.
CP. p. 42.

LETTERS TO A PSYCHIATRIST (includes the following poems:)
Christmas Letter (five poems)
Contempora. 2 (September/February, 1972), 24-25.
DF. pp. 69-71.
CP. pp. 400-402.
The Fear of Angels
DF. p. 72.
CP. pp. 402-403.
The Action of Therapy (six poems)
Beloit Poetry Journal. 22 (Fall-Winter, 1971-1972), 7-12.
DF. p. 78.
CP. p. 408.
I Speak of Change
The Small Pond, Fall, 1971, p. 22. (variant title: "Illumination Exists")
DF. p. 78.
CP. p. 408.
Easter 1971
The Small Pond, Fall, 1971, p. 22.
DF. p. 79.
CP. p. 409.

LETTERS TO MYSELF (two poems)
Virginia Quarterly Review. 42 (Summer, 1966), 404-405.

LIFTING STONE
Cornhill Magazine. 168 (Spring, 1956), 352.
ITLA. p. 57.
CSSV. p. 66.
CP. p. 186.

A LIGHT LEFT ON
Recurrence. 2 (Spring, 1952), 12.
LoS. p. 53.
Modern Love Poems. ed., D. J. Klemer, New York: Doubleday, 1961, p. 66.
CP. p. 136.

THE LIGHT YEARS
ITLA. p. 69.

CSSV. p. 77.
Harvard Poetry Reading (D 868.1/9) October 10, 1962.
CP. p. 194.

LINCOLN MEMORIAL
New York Herald Tribune, February 10, 1949, p. 28.

LION AND THE ROSE
(From the sequence entitled "Theme and Variation: Santa Fe, New Mexico")
Poetry. 68 (May, 1946), 74-78.
L&R. p. 8.
CSSV. p. 93.
CP. p. 571.

LITERAL NOW, THE TREMBLING AND THE FEAR/
(From the sequence entitled "Over Troubled Water")
Francis Marion Review. 1 (1975), 12.

LOSE THE PAIN IN THE SNOW
(Under the heading "Two Songs")
Poetry. 74 (August, 1949), 271-272.
LoS. p. 84. (variant reading)

LOVE CANNOT ACT, AND SO I MUST EMBARK/
(From the sequence entitled "Over Troubled Water")
Francis Marion Review. 1 (1975), 13.

LOVE, FALL AS LIGHTLY ON HIS LIDS AS SLEEP/
Poetry. 43 (October 27, 1933), 27. (under the title "Antelope")
EiA. p. 67.

LOVERS AT THE ZOO
Literary Review. 7 (Summer, 1964), 562-563.
PM. p. 88.
CP. p. 285.

LULLABY
LoT. p. 26.
LoS. p. 51.
CP. p. 107.

MAGNET
L&R. p. 71.

MAP FOR DESPAIR
IL. p. 59.

MARCH IN NEW ENGLAND
Pennsylvania Literary Review. 8 (1957), 8.
DF. p. 53.
CP. p. 392.

MARCH-MAD
Yankee, March, 1966, p. 152.
ADNH. p. 25.
CP. p. 304.

MAY WALK
DF. p. 23.

MEDITATION IN SUNLIGHT
(From the sequence entitled "Theme and Variation: Santa Fe, New Mexico")
Poetry. 68 (May, 1946), 74-78.
L&R. p. 3.
CSSV. p. 19.
CP. p. 54.

MEDITERRANEAN
New Yorker. 31 (October 20, 1955), 120.
ITLA. p. 36.
CP. p. 174.

MEMORY OF SWANS
IL. p. 35.
Harvard Poetry Reading (D 13. 3/2,3,4) August 6, 1941.
CP. p. 36.

METAMORPHOSIS
Ladies Home Journal. 73 (May, 1956), 175.
ADNH. p. 26.
CP. p. 305.

THE METAPHYSICAL GARDEN
Botteghe Oscure. 14 (1954), 273-276.
CSSV. p. 53.
CP. p. 163.

MINTING TIME
New York Herald Tribune, November 9, 1958, p. 4.
Cornhill Magazine. 171 (Winter, 1959-1960), 101-103.
ADNH. p. 42.

MONTICELLO
Harvard Poetry Reading (D 13. 3/2,3,4) August 6, 1941.

Decision. 2 (October, 1941), 18.
L&R. p. 15.
CSSV. p. 28.
CP. p. 4.

MOTH IN THE SCHOOLROOM
DF. p. 28.

MOUNTAIN INTERVAL (includes the following poems:)
Landscape
EiA. p. 42.
Interval
EiA. p. 43.
Image
EiA. p. 43-44.
Japanese Print
EiA. p. 44.
The Bridge
EiA. p. 45-46.

MOVING IN
Massachusetts Review. 1 (February, 1960), 343.
CSSV. p. 135.
CP. p. 210.
To Be Alone. ed., Joan Berg Victor, New York: Crown Publishers, 1974, p. 24.

MOZART AGAIN
DF. p. 22.
CP. p. 370.

MUD SEASON
CSSV. p. 138.
ADNH. p. 24.
CP. p. 213.

THE MUSE AS MEDUSA
Ante. 3 (Summer, 1967), 63.
GoMS. p. 38.
CP. p. 332.

MY FATHER'S DEATH
Harper's Magazine. 214 (April, 1957), 82.
ITLA. p. 66.
CSSV. p. 102.
CP. p. 193.

MY SISTERS, O MY SISTERS (1-4)
L&R. p. 56.
CP. p. 74.

MYSELF TO ME
DF. p. 17.
CP. p. 365.

MYTH
LoT. p. 9.
LoS. p. 65.
CP. p. 99.

NARCISSUS
LoS. p. 88.

NATIVITY
New Poems by American Poets #2. ed., Rolfe Humphries, New York: Ballantine Books, 1957, p. 137.
ITLA. p. 51.
CSSV. p. 106.
Garlands for Christmas. ed., Chad Walsh, New York: Macmillan, 1965, pp. 53-54.
CP. p. 183.

NAVIGATOR
New Yorker. 19 (February 29, 1943), 22.
L&R. p. 90.
CP. p. 88.

NEVER IS SILENCE CRUEL, NO, / (variant reading, see SILENCE IS NEVER CRUEL, NO, /)
Poetry. 74 (August, 1949), 272-273.
LoS. p. 85.

THE NEW TOURIST
LoS. p. 21.

NEW YEAR WISHES
L&R. p. 39.
Modern Religious Poems. ed., Jacob Trapp, New York: Harper & Row, 1964, p. 251.

NIGHT STORM
Atlantic Monthly. 176 (December, 1945), 90.
L&R. p. 46.

NIGHT WATCH
The Small Pond, Fall, 1969, pp. 33-38.
GoMS. pp. 27-30.
CP. p. 324-327.

NO, I WILL NEVER FORGET YOU (SONG)
Life and Letters Today. 42 (September, 1944), 160.
L&R. p. 42.

NO SPRING CAN BE ETERNAL, NOR CAN THIS/
(From the sequence entitled "Portraits of Three Women")
Poetry. 40 (April, 1932), 14.
EiA. p. 7.

NO WORD OF LOVER EVER WAS SO BRIEF/
(From the sequence entitled "Portraits of Three Women")
EiA. p. 38-39.

A NOBLEMAN'S HOUSE
PM. p. 27.
CP. p. 233.

A NORTHERNER SEES THE COTTONFIELDS FOR THE FIRST TIME
(From the sequence entitled "American Notebook")
Poetry. 59 (February, 1942), 240-241.

NOSTALGIA FOR INDIA
PM. p. 50.
CP. p. 254.

NOT ALWAYS THE QUIET WORD
L&R. p. 88.

NOT FOR MY SAKE WHO HAVE DESIRED IT SO/
IL. p. 15.

NOT WITHOUT GRACE AND CERTAINLY WITH PRIDE/
(From the sequence entitled "Encounter in April")
EiA. p. 9.

NOTE TO A PHOTOGRAPHER
DF. p. 52.
CP. p. 391.

NOTES FROM INDIA (includes the following poems:)
At Bhubaneswar
Texas Quarterly. 7 (Summer, 1964), 64-66.

PM. pp. 38-40.
CP. pp. 244-246.
At Kanarak
Texas Quarterly. 7 (Summer, 1964), 66-67.
PM. pp. 40-41.
CP. pp. 246-247.
At Puri
Texas Quarterly. 7 (Summer, 1964), 67-68.
PM. pp. 41-42.
CP. pp. 247-248.
At Fathpur Sikri
PM. p. 42.
CP. p. 248.

NOW I BECOME MYSELF
Harvard Poetry Reading (T 851.1/1) no date
Atlantic Monthly. 182 (December, 1948), 42.
LoS. p. 99.
CSSV. p. 95.
CP. p. 156.

NOW IT IS EVENING COMING AND YOU ARE NOT HERE/
(From the sequence entitled "Canticles")
IL. p. 49.

NOW LET ME REST. NOW LET ME LAY MY HAND/
EiA. p. 81.

NOW THAT EVENING GATHERS UP THE DAY/
(From the sequence entitled "These Images Remain")
LoS. p. 68.
Modern Love Poems. ed., D. J. Klemer, New York: Doubleday, 1961, p. 31.
CP. p. 144.

NOW VOYAGER
L&R. p. 55.
Harvard Poetry Reading (T 830.9/2) March 26, 1951.
CSSV. p. 74.
CP. p. 73.

NURSERY RHYME
EiA. p. 31.

O SAISONS! O CHATEAUX!
L&R. p. 77.
CSSV. p. 42.
CP. p. 82.

O THAT I WERE AS GREAT AS IS MY GRIEF/
University Review. (University of Kansas City) 12 (Spring, 1946), 214-215.

O WHO CAN TELL
Harvard Poetry Reading (T 851.1/1) no date
L&R. p. 46.
New York Times Book Review, July 10, 1949, p. 2.
CP. p. 68.

AN OBSERVATION
Voices. 178 (May-August, 1962), 28-29.
PM. p. 71.
ADNH. p. 30.
CP. p. 271.

OF FRIENDSHIP
LoS. p. 47.

OF GRIEF
DF. p. 62.
CP. p. 395.

OF HAVENS
Literary Review. 7 (Autumn, 1963), 6.
PM. p. 66.
ADNH. p. 55.
CP. p. 266.

OF PRAYER
Botteghe Oscure. 9 (1952), 293-294.
LoS. p. 39.
CP. p. 133.

OF THE MUSE
Virginia Quarterly Review. 42 (Summer, 1966), 402.

OF THE SEASONS (SANGRE DE CRISTO MOUNTAINS, SANTA FE, NEW MEXICO)
(From the sequence entitled "American Notebook")
Harvard Poetry Reading (D 13.3/2,3,4) August 6, 1941.
Poetry. 59 (February, 1942), 240-241.
L&R. p. 24.
Archive of Recorded Poetry and Literature. Washington, D.C.: U.S. Library of Congress, 1961.
CP. p. 53.

OH CHILD LOOK DOWN, LOOK DOWN YOUR OPEN EYES/
IL. p. 18.

OHIO COUNTRY
(From the sequence entitled "American Notebook")
Poetry. 59 (February, 1942), 239-240.

OLD SONG
Atlantic Monthly. 164 (August, 1939), 258.
Anthology of Magazine Verse and Yearbook of American Poetry for 1938-1941. ed., Alan F. Pater, New York: Paebar Company, 1942, p. 414.

THE OLIVE GROVE
New Yorker. 31 (August 13, 1955), 27.
ITLA. p. 35.
CSSV. p. 38.
CP. p. 173.

ON A WINTER NIGHT
Voices. 151 (May-August, 1953), 24-25.
New York Herald Tribune, July 5, 1953, p. 4.
LoS. p. 97.
Archive of Recorded Poetry and Literature. Washington, D. C.: U. S. Library of Congress, 1961.
CSSV. p. 94.
Harvard Poetry Reading (D 868.1/9) October 10, 1962.
CP. p. 155.

ON BEING GIVEN TIME
Archive of Recorded Poetry and Literature. Washington, D. C.: U. S. Library of Congress, 1961.
CSSV. p. 59.
Harvard Poetry Reading (D 868.1/9) October 10, 1962.
CP. p. 164.

ON HAMPSHIRE DOWNS
EiA. p. 30.

ON PATMOS
PM. p. 53.
CP. p. 255.

ON THE ATLANTIC
EiA. p. 25.

ONCE MORE AT CHARTRES
The Lyric. 46 (Fall, 1966), 81.
GoMS. p. 63.
CP. p. 349.

THE OTHER PLACE
ITLA. p. 64.
CP. p. 189.

OUT OF DEEP WELLS OF SLEEP ALL NIGHT THEY ROSE/
(From the sequence entitled "These Images Remain")
LoS. p. 72.

OVER TROUBLED WATER (includes the following sonnets:)
Francis Marion Review. 1 (1975), 11-17.
I sit at my desk in a huge silence/ p. 11.
Everywhere, in my garden, in my thought/ p. 11.
Literal now, the trembling and the fear,/ p. 12.
The poet dances on a rope held taut/ p. 12.
Love cannot act, and so I must embark,/ p. 13.
We know the legend of clear loving eyes/ p. 13.
The legend haunts us still. Each of us wears/ p. 14.
Constrained it can be. Short of death/ p. 14.
If you take refuge in a word then bear/ p. 15.
Last night I stood beside you in your hell,/ p. 15.
It's the time of breaking, your house sold,/ p. 16.
So there was, after all, no destination/ p. 16.
We got off where we started months ago/ p. 17.

PAIR OF HANDS
New York Times Book Review, December 2, 1956, p. 2.
Atlantic Monthly. 198 (September, 1965), 63.
ITLA. p. 66.
CSSV. p. 75.
CP. p. 192.

A PARROT
GoMS. p. 49.
CP. p. 341.

PASSION LIKE RADIUM IS LUMINOUS IN ESSENCE/
(From the sequence entitled "Canticles")
IL. p. 40.

PASTORAL
PM. p. 59.

PAVILION
Niagara Falls Gazette, June 15, 1940, p. 26.

PERSPECTIVE
L&R. p. 75.
CP. p. 80

THE PHOENIX
Hudson Review. 9 (Spring, 1956), 44-45.
ITLA. p. 44.
Archive of Recorded Poetry and Literature. Washington, D.C.: U.S. Library of Congress, 1961.
CSSV. p. 89.
CP. p. 181.

PLANT DREAMING DEEP (See also: HEUREUX QUI, COMME ULYSSE)
ADNH. p. 56.

POEM IN AUTUMN
Atlantic Monthly. 170 (December, 1942), 42.
L&R. p. 54.

THE POET DANCES ON A ROPE HELD TAUT/
(From the sequence entitled "Over Troubled Water")
Francis Marion Review. 1 (1975), 12.

POET IN RESIDENCE (Also appeared as a reprint, Southern Illinois University/Department of English, 1948.) (includes the following poems:)
The Students
L&R. p. 30.
CP. p. 61.
Campus
L&R. pp. 31-32.
CP. p. 62.
Before Teaching
L&R. pp. 32-33.
Shady Hill News, February, 1959, p. 3.
CP. p. 63.
After Teaching
L&R. p. 33-34.
CP. p. 63.
Place of Learning
L&R. pp. 35-36.
CP. p. 64.

POETS AND THE RAIN
LoT. pp. 34-35.
LoS. p. 95.
CP. p. 110.

THE POPPY
LoT. p. 13.

PORTRAIT BY HOLBEIN
EiA. p. 35.

PORTRAIT OF ONE PERSON
EiA. p. 36.

PORTRAIT OF THE ARTIST
EiA. p. 37.

PORTRAITS OF THREE WOMEN (includes the following poems:)
I have watched time falling across your hair/
EiA. p. 38.
No word of lover ever was so brief/
EiA. pp. 38-39.
Your little head would not have pleased the Greeks/
EiA. p. 39.

PRAYER BEFORE WORK
IL. p. 3.
Archive of Recorded Poetry and Literature. Washington, D. C.: U. S. Library of Congress, 1961.
CP. p. 31.

THE PRIDE OF TREES
IL. p. 61.

PRISONER AT A DESK
Poetry. 119 (February, 1972), 269.
DF. p. 64.
CP. p. 397.

THE PRIVATE FACE IS SCREAMING (AT ANY WRITER'S CONFERENCE)
Beloit Poetry Journal. 2 (Spring, 1952), 4.

PROTEUS
Harvard Poetry Reading (D 868.1/9) October 10, 1962.
GoMS. p. 33.
CP. p. 329.

PROTHALAMION

New Poems by American Poets. ed., Rolfe Humphries, New York: Ballantine Books, 1953, p. 135.
LoS. p. 61.
CSSV. p. 70.
High Wedlock Then Be Honoured. ed., Virginia Tufts, New York: Viking Press, 1970, p. 279.
CP. p. 141.

PROVENCE

New Yorker. 29 (June 20, 1953), 30.
LoS. p. 14.
New York Times, August 29, 1954, p. 2.
CSSV. p. 36.
Archive of Recorded Poetry and Literature. Washington, D.C.: U.S. Library of Congress, 1961.
CP. p. 121.

THE PURITAN

IL. p. 54.

QUESTION

Briarcliff Quarterly. 2 (April, 1945), 23.
L&R. p. 72.
CP. p. 79.

THE REAL CONFLICT IS DEATH AND THAT IS WHY/
(From the sequence entitled "These Images Remain")

LoS. p. 73.

A RECOGNITION

Yankee, January, 1965, p. 116.
PM. p. 103.
ADNH. p. 34.
CP. p. 295.

RECORD

IL. p. 7.

REEDS AND WATER

DF. p. 27.
CP. p. 373.

REFLECTED TREE

LoS. p. 13.
New York Times Book Review, September 5, 1954, p. 2.

REFLECTIONS BY A FIRE
Cornhill Magazine. 169 (Summer, 1957), 263-264.
ITLA. p. 71.
Harvard Poetry Reading (D 868.1/9) October 10, 1962.
CP. p. 197.

REQUEST
EiA. p. 49.

RETURN
L&R. p. 76.
CP. p. 81.

THE RETURN OF APHRODITE
DF. p. 19.
CP. p. 367.

RETURN TO CHARTRES
Atlantic Monthly. 180 (December, 1947), 126.

THE ROCK IN THE SNOWBALL
GoMS. p. 13.
CP. p. 315.

ROMAN HEAD
L&R. p. 89.
CSSV. p. 40.

THE ROSE HAS OPENED AND IS ALL ACCOMPLISHED/
(From the sequence entitled "These Images Remain")
LoS. p. 71.
CP. p. 145.

ROSES
LoS. p. 6.

SACRED ORDER
Life and Letters Today. 31 (November, 1941), 129-130.
Studies and Essays in the History of Science and Learning in Honor of George Sarton. ed., Ashley Montague, New York: R. Schuman, 1946, p. 595.
L&R. p. 85.
Shady Hill News, February, 1959, p. 2.
Imagination's Other Place. ed., Helen Plotz, New York: Thomas Y. Crowell, 1955, p. 155.
CP. p. 86.

SACRED WOOD

Poetry. 81 (January, 1953), 232-233.
LoS. p. 3.
CSSV. p. 65.
CP. p. 116.

SANTOS: NEW MEXICO

Harvard Poetry Reading (D 13.3/2,3,4) August 6, 1941.
Atlantic Monthly. 170 (December, 1942), 60.
The Best Poems of 1943. ed., Thomas Moult, New York: Harcourt, Brace, 1944, pp. 53-54.
The Questing Spirit. eds., Halford Luccock and Frances Brentano, New York: Coward-McCann, Inc., 1947, p. 277.
L&R. p. 28.
Harvard Poetry Reading (T 830.9/2) March 26, 1951.
The Earth Is the Lord's: Poems of the Spirit. ed., Helen Plotz, New York: Thomas Y. Crowell, 1965, p. 116.
CP. p. 60.
The Choice Is Always Ours. ed., Dorothy Phillips, New York: Pyramid Books, 1975, p. 123.

SAY IT IS WELL

Ladies Home Journal. 68 (October, 1951), 224.

THE SEAS OF WHEAT

LoS. p. 65.
CP. p. 143.

SECOND SPRING

Harvard Poetry Reading (T 851.1/1) no date
Harvard Poetry Reading (T 830.9/2) March 26, 1951.
LoT. p. 14.
CP. p. 102.

SECOND THOUGHTS ON THE ABSTRACT GARDENS OF JAPAN

Transatlantic Review. 15 (Spring, 1964), 47-49.
PM. p. 78.
CP. p. 278.

SESTINA
(From the sequence entitled "Three Poems")

Poetry. 65 (February, 1945), 231-233.

SHE SHALL BE CALLED WOMAN

EiA. pp. 13-22.
CP. pp. 20-26.

SHUGAKU-IN, IMPERIAL VILLA
PM. p. 26.

THE SILENCE
Green River Review. 2 (Spring, 1970), 15-16.
GoMS. p. 59.
CP. p. 346.

SILENCE IS NEVER CRUEL/ (variant reading, see NEVER IS SILENCE CRUEL, NO,/)
Poetry. 74 (August, 1949), 272-273.
LoS. p. 85.

SIMPLE FUGUE
Pennsylvania Literary Review. 8 (1957), 8.

SINCE I AM WHAT I AM, AN INCOMPLETE/
EiA. p. 71.

THE SLEEPING GOD
PM. p. 46.
CP. p. 250.

SLIGHT DEATH
EiA. p. 60.

THE SNOW LIGHT
DF. p. 29.
CP. p. 374.

SO THERE WAS, AFTER ALL, NO DESTINATION/
(From the sequence entitled "Over Troubled Water")
Francis Marion Review. 1 (1975), 17.

SO TO RELEASE THE SOUL, SEARCH OUT THE SOUL/
(From the sequence entitled "These Images Remain")
LoS. p. 70.
CP. p. 144.

SOMERSAULT
ITLA. p. 41.
CSSV. p. 92.
CP. p. 179.

SOMEWHERE THERE IS DELIGHT LOVE WILL NOT BRING/
EiA. p. 75.

SONG: COME LET US DANCE MY LOVE/
Nation. 182 (April 14, 1956), 350.
ITLA. p. 62.

SONG FOR A MARRIAGE
Ladies Home Journal. 71 (August, 1954), 110.

SONG FOR DROUGHT
EiA. p. 62.

SONG IN AUTUMN
New York Herald Tribune, October 26, 1948, p. 28.
LoT. p. 37.

SONG: IT IS STILL YOU WHO/
Saturday Review of Literature. 13 (October 30, 1948), 17.
LoT. p. 38.
LoS. p. 87.

SONG: LOSE THE PAIN IN THE SNOW see LOSE THE PAIN IN THE SNOW

SONG: NOW LET US HONOR WITH VIOLIN AND FLUTE
L&R. p. 48.
Modern Religious Poems. ed., Jacob Trapp, New York: Harper & Row, 1964, p. 175.
CP. p. 70.

SONG: WHEN I IMAGINE WHAT TO GIVE YOU/
L&R. p. 70.

SONG WITHOUT MUSIC
LoT. p. 10.
CP. p. 100.

SOUNDS
Harvard Poetry Reading (T 851.1/1) no date.
LoT. p. 11.

THE SPIRIT COMES BACK TO SILENCE LIKE A DOVE/
(From the sequence entitled "Canticles")
IL. p. 47.

SPRING AIR
New York Herald Tribune, April 30, 1952, p. 18.

SPRING CHORUS

Choral Speaking in the English Course. comp., Cecile De Banke, Massachusetts: Walter H. Baker Co., 1943.

SPRING DAY

Atlantic Monthly. 199 (April, 1957), 73.
ITLA. p. 68.
CSSV. p. 76.
CP. p. 195.

SPRING PLANTING

Poetry/London-New York. 1 (Winter, 1957), 11-12.
Best Poems of 1958. Palo Alto: Pacific Books, 1960, p. 88.
CSSV. p. 139.
CP. p. 214.

SPRING SONG

L&R. p. 67.

STATIC LANDSCAPE

IL. p. 56.

STILL LIFE IN SNOWSTORM

Yankee, April, 1964, p. 156.
PM. p. 68.
ADNH. p. 28.
CP. p. 268.

THE STONE GARDEN

Colorado Quarterly. 14 (Spring, 1966), 305-306.
PM. p. 32.
CP. p. 238.

THE STONE RESISTS

Harvard Poetry Reading (T 851.1/1) no date.
Beloit Poetry Journal. 1 (1950), 31.
LoS. p. 75.
CP. p. 238. (variant reading)

STONE WALLS

ADNH. p. 49.
CP. p. 308.

A STORM OF ANGELS

DF. p. 33.
CP. p. 378.

STRANGERS
EiA. p. 83.
CP. p. 27.

SUMMARY
IL. p. 28.
CP. p. 34.

SUMMER MUSIC
New Poems by American Poets. ed., Rolfe Humphries, New York: Ballantine Books, 1953, p. 134.
LoS. p. 7.
CSSV. p. 33.
CP. p. 117.
New Coasts and Strange Harbors: Discovering Poems. eds., Helen Hill and Agnes Perkins, New York: Thomas Y. Crowell, 1974, p. 91.

SUMMER NIGHT
LoT. p. 15

SUN BOAT
Colorado Quarterly. 4 (Spring, 1956), 357.
ITLA. p. 53.
CSSV. p. 60.

THE SURFERS
DF. p. 31.
CP. p. 376.

THE SWANS
LoT. p. 12.
LoS. p. 10.
CSSV. p. 69.
Harvard Poetry Reading (D868.1/9) October 10, 1962.
CP. p. 101.

TAKE ANGUISH FOR COMPANION
LoS. p. 25.
CSSV. p. 115.
CP. p. 127.

THE TEACHERS
Queen's Quarterly. 52 (Autumn, 1945), 279.
Ladies Home Journal. 70 (January, 1953), 66. (only the last three stanzas)

A TEAM PLOUGHING
Yankee, May, 1966, p. 164.

THAT NIGHT WE WENT OUTSIDE THE GATE BEYOND THE WOOD/
(From the sequence entitled "Canticles")
IL. p. 45.

THEME AND VARIATION: SANTA FE, NEW MEXICO (includes the following poems:)
Meditation in Sunlight
Poetry. 68 (May, 1946), 74-75.
L&R. pp. 3-4.
The Window
Poetry. 68 (May, 1946), 75-76.
L&R. p. 7.
Difficult Scene
Poetry. 68 (May, 1946), 76-77.
L&R. pp. 5-6.
The Lion and the Rose
Poetry. 68 (May, 1946), 77-78.
L&R. pp. 8-9.

THERE ARE VOICES IN THE GARDEN. DAY FOLDS ITSELF INTO/
(From the sequence entitled "Canticles")
IL. p. 46.

THERE COMES A MOMENT WHEN THE GENTLE FLESH/
EiA. p. 77.

THERE IS NO STRENGTH OF WORDS, NONE HARD AND PURE/
IL. p. 23.

THESE IMAGES REMAIN (includes the following sonnets:)
Now that the evening gathers up the day, /
LoS. p. 68.
Modern Love Poems. ed., D. J. Klemer, New York: Doubleday, 1961, p. 31.
CP. p. 144.
Even such fervor must seek out an end, /
LoS. p. 69.
Modern Love Poems. ed., D. J. Klemer, New York: Doubleday, 1961, p. 31.
CP. p. 144.

So to release the soul, search out the soul/
LoS. p. 70.
CP. p. 144.
The rose has opened and is all accomplished/
LoS. p. 71.
CP. p. 145.
Out of deep wells of sleep all night they rose,/
LoS. p. 72.
The real conflict is death and that is why/
LoS. p. 73.
But parting is return, the coming home,/
Atlantic Monthly. 183 (March, 1949), 58-59.
LoS. p. 74.
CP. p. 145.
The stone resists: the chisel does destroy,/
LoS. p. 75.
CP. p. 74. (variant reading)
What angel can I leave, gentle and stern/
Atlantic Monthly. 183 (March, 1949), 59.
LoS. p. 76.
CP. p. 146.
These images remain, these classic landscapes/
Atlantic Monthly. 183 (March, 1949), 58.
LoS. p. 77.
CP. p. 146.
Here are the peaceful days we never knew./
Atlantic Monthly. 183 (March, 1949), 58.
LoS. p. 78.
CP. p. 147.
Here let me lie, quiet upon your shoulder,/
Atlantic Monthly. 183 (March, 1949), 59.

THESE PURE ARCHES
Saturday Review of Literature. 28 (August 25, 1945), 26.
L&R. p. 81.
Harvard Poetry Reading (T 830.9/2) March 26, 1951.
CSSV. p. 121.
CP. p. 83.

THESE WERE HER NIGHTLY JOURNEYS
ITLA. p. 33. (under the title "The Fall")
CSSV. p. 90.
CP. p. 171.

THEY ALSO
(From the sequence entitled "Words on the Wind")
Poetry. 37 (December, 1930), 145-146.

THINGS SEEN
DF. p. 21.
CP. p. 369.

THIS WAS OUR TESTING YEAR AFTER THE FIRST
(From the sequence entitled "The Autumn Sonnets")
DF. p. 46.
CP. p. 388.

THREE POEMS (includes the following poems:)
Poetry. 65 (February, 1945), 231-240.
Sestina, pp. 231-233.
Homage to Flanders, pp. 233-234.
To the Living, pp. 235-240.

TIGER
Atlantic Monthly. 186 (November, 1950), 63.
LoS. p. 31.

TO AN ANGEL
Beloit Poetry Journal. 1 (Summer, 1951), 5-6.

TO AN HONEST FRIEND
LoT. p. 22.
LoS. p. 49.
CP. p. 104.

TO STAND ON THE EARTH AGAIN IS A GRAVE EVENT/
(From the sequence entitled "Canticles")
IL. p. 44.

TO THE LIVING
Poetry. 65 (February, 1945), 235-240.
L&R. p. 94.
Harvard Poetry Reading (T 830.9/2) March 26, 1951. (excerpt)
Shady Hill News, February, 1959, pp. 3-4. (Part 2 only)
CSSV. p. 117.
CP. p. 91.
Voices of Protest and Hope. comp., Elizabeth Dodds, New York: Friendship Press, 1965, p. 139. (excerpt)

TO THE NORTH
Cornhill Magazine. 169 (Winter, 1957-1958), 468.
ITLA. p. 38.
CSSV. p. 41.
CP. p. 176.

TO THE WEARY
EiA. p. 63.

THE TORTURED
University Review. (University of Kansas City) 12 (Spring, 1946), 214.
L&R. p. 99.
CSSV. p. 112.
War: An Anthology. eds., Edward Huberman and Elizabeth Huberman, New York: Washington Square Press, 1969.
Enough of Dying! eds., Kay Boyle and Justine Van Gurday, New York: Dell, 1972, pp. 293-294.
CP. p. 95.

TRANSITION
IL. p. 32.
New Poems by American Poets. ed., Rolfe Humphries, New York: Ballantine Books, 1953, p. 137.

TRANSITIONS
LoS. p. 9.
CP. p. 119.

TRANSLATION
IL. p. 33.

THE TREE
Saturday Review of Literature. 35 (December 27, 1952), 21.
LoS. p. 41.
CSSV. p. 107.
CP. p. 135.

THE TREE IN THE CLOUD
Ladies Home Journal. 67 (December, 1950), 167.

THE TREE PEONY
DF. p. 24.
CP. p. 371.

THE TREES
EiA. p. 27.

TROUBADOUR SONG
EiA. p. 61.

TROUBLE IN CAMBRIDGE
<u>The New Republic</u>. 111 (August 28, 1944), 246.

TRUTH
<u>Saturday Review of Literature</u>. 32 (December 31, 1949), 18.
<u>LoT</u>. p. 23.
<u>LoS</u>. p. 50.

TURTLE
<u>Cornhill Magazine</u>. 174 (Winter, 1964-1965), 293-294.
<u>PM</u>. p. 89

TWICE I HAVE SET MY HEART UPON A SHARING/
(From the sequence entitled "The Autumn Sonnets")
<u>DF</u>. p. 45.
<u>CP</u>. p. 387.

TWO SICK KITTENS
<u>Cat Fancy Magazine</u>. 15 (November-December, 1972), 16.
<u>A Celebration of Cats</u>. ed., Jean Burden, New York: Paul Eriksson, 1974, p. 32.

TWO SONGS (includes the following poems:)
Lose the Pain in the Snow
<u>Poetry</u>. 74 (August, 1949), 271-272.
<u>LoS</u>. p. 84 (variant reading)
Silence is never cruel, no/ (variant reading)
<u>Poetry</u>. 74 (August, 1949), 272-273.
<u>LoS</u>. p. 85.

UNDER THE LEAVES AN INFANT LOVE LIES DEAD/
(From the sequence entitled "The Autumn Sonnets")
<u>DF</u>. p. 43.
<u>CP</u>. p. 385.

UNDERSTATEMENT
<u>IL</u>. p. 9.
<u>CP</u>. p. 33

UNLUCKY SOLDIER
<u>Atlantic Monthly</u>. 174 (August, 1944), 102.
<u>L&R</u>. p. 91.

THE VANQUISHED
<u>London Mercury</u>. 36 (September, 1937), 419.
<u>IL</u>. p. 34.

A VILLAGE TALE
Kenyon Review. 23 (Spring, 1961), 274-275.
Harvard Poetry Reading (D 868.1/9) October 10, 1962.
PM. p. 83.
CP. p. 280.

VILLANELLE FOR FIREWORKS
LoS. p. 12.
CP. p. 120.

VILLANELLE 1941
Decision. I (May, 1941), 43.

A VISION OF HOLLAND
Contempora. 1 (October/November, 1970), 35.
GoMS. p. 44.
CP. p. 338.

THE WALLED GARDEN AT CLONDALKIN
Poetry. 85 (March, 1955), 344-346.
PM. p. 100.
CP. p. 292.

WARNING
DF. p. 30.
CP. p. 375.

THE WATER MEADOWS
Ladies Home Journal. 68 (June, 1951), 150.

THE WAVES
Voices. 172 (May-August, 1960), 31-32.
GoMS. p. 68.
CP. p. 354.

WE CAME TOGETHER SOFTLY LIKE TWO DEER/
(From the sequence entitled "Encounter in April")
Poetry. 40 (April, 1932), 14.
EiA. p. 7.

WE GOT OFF WHERE WE STARTED MONTHS AGO/
(From the sequence entitled "Over Troubled Water")
Francis Marion Review. 1 (1975), 17.

WE HAVE SEEN THE WIND
Saturday Review of Literature. 19 (February 4, 1939), 8.
L&R. p. 82.

ADNH. p. 48.
CP. p. 84.

WE KNOW THE LEGEND OF CLEAR LOVING EYES/
(From the sequence entitled "Over Troubled Water")
Francis Marion Review. 1 (1975), 13.

WE SAT SMOKING AT A TABLE BY THE RIVER/
(From the sequence entitled "Canticles")
IL. p. 48.
CP. p. 38.

WE SHALL REMEMBER THE LAKE
LoT. p. 16.

WE WATCHED THE WATERFALLS, RICH AND BAROQUE/
(From the sequence entitled "The Autumn Sonnets")
DF. p. 46.
CP. p. 388-389.

WE WHO HAD BEEN SO WOUNDED AND SO CLOVEN/
EiA. p. 74.

WEEK END
EiA. p. 28.

WE'LL TO THE WOODS NO MORE, THE LAURELS ARE CUT DOWN: AT KENT STATE
GoMS. p. 26.
CP. p. 323.

WHAT ANGEL CAN I LEAVE, GENTLE AND STERN/
(From the sequence entitled "These Images Remain")
Atlantic Monthly. 183 (March, 1949), 59.
LoS. p. 76.
CP. p. 146.

WHAT THE OLD MAN SAID
Poetry. 57 (December, 1940), 176.
L&R. p. 87.
CSSV. p. 114.
CP. p. 87.

WHEN IN THE LIGHT-STORMED AND ARIEL CITY/
Virginia Quarterly Review. 35 (Summer, 1959), 410.
The Various Light. eds., Leah Bodine Drake and Charles Arthur Muses, Switzerland: Aurora Press, 1964, p. 305.

WHERE DREAM BEGINS
ITLA. p. 27.
Archive of Recorded Poetry and Literature. Washington, D. C.: U. S. Library of Congress, 1961.
CP. p. 168.

WHERE THE GRASSES (EASTERN KANSAS)
(From the sequence entitled "American Notebook")
Poetry. 59 (February, 1942), 235-237.

WHERE THE PEACOCK CRIED
L&R. p. 18.
CP. p. 49.

WHERE THOUGHT LEAPS ON
Ladies Home Journal. 75 (February, 1958), 140.

WHERE WARRIORS STOOD
New York Herald Tribune, November 24, 1948, p. 20.
LoS. p. 24.
CSSV. p. 113.
CP. p. 126.

WHILE THE GREAT MOON RISES
Ladies Home Journal. 68 (May, 1951), 231.

THE WHITE-HAIRED MAN (FOR RICHARD CABOT)
L&R. p. 49.
Modern Religious Poems. ed., Jacob Trapp, New York: Harper & Row, 1964, p. 173.

WHO WAKES: DETROIT, JUNE, 1943
The New Republic. 109 (August 16, 1943), 222.
L&R. p. 92.
CSSV. p. 11.
CP. p. 89.

WINCHESTER, VIRGINIA
L&R. p. 13.
CSSV. p. 26.

THE WIND WHICH SWEPT THE EARTH HAS MOUNTED THE TREES/
(From the sequence entitled "Canticles")
IL. p. 41.

THE WINDOW
(From the sequence entitled "Theme and Variation: Santa Fe,

New Mexico")
Poetry. 68 (May, 1946), 75-76.
L&R. p. 7.
Harvard Poetry Reading (T 830.9/2) March 26, 1951.
CP. p. 56.

WINTER CAROL
DF. p. 57.

WINTER EVENING
IL. p. 58.
CP. p. 41.

WINTER GRACE
New York Times Book Review, October 8, 1950, p. 2.
LoT. p. 39.
LoS. p. 43.
CP. p. 112.

WINTER LIGHT
Pennsylvania Literary Review. 8 (1957), 7.

WINTER NIGHT
Yankee, February, 1967, p. 148.
ADNH. p. 18.
CP. p. 303.

WITHOUT THE VIOLENCE
Harper's Magazine. 201 (July, 1950), 78.
LoS. p. 81.
CSSV. p. 21.
CP. p. 148.

WOOD, PAPER, STONE
PM. p. 34.
CP. p. 240.

WORD FROM LIMBO (FOR MY STUDENTS)
Virginia Quarterly Review. 42 (Summer, 1966), 407-409.

WORDS ON THE WIND (includes the following poems:)
Poetry. 97 (December, 1930), 144-146.
Let No Wind Come, p. 145.
First Love, p. 144.
Fruit of Loneliness, p. 146.
They Also, pp. 145-146.

WORK OF HAPPINESS
Atlantic Monthly. 178 (July, 1946), 108.
L&R. p. 43.
CSSV. p. 62.
Modern Religious Poems. ed., Jacob Trapp, New York: Harper & Row, 1964, pp. 246-247.
ADNH. p. 33.
CP. p. 66.

YET PLUCK OUT FROM THIS NETTLE A BRAVE FLOWER/
IL. p. 25.

YOU HAD FOUND WORDS FOR THIS AND CALLED IT LOVE/
EiA. p. 69.

YOU WHO ASK FOR PEACE
IL. p. 60.

YOUR LITTLE HEAD WOULD NOT HAVE PLEASED THE GREEKS
(From the sequence entitled "Portraits of Three Women")
EiA. p. 39.

SELECTED BIBLIOGRAPHY OF REFERENCE SOURCES

Abstracts of English Studies. Ed. Lewis Sawin. Urbana, Ill.: National Council of Teachers of English, 1959-1973.

American Authors and Books of 1640 to the Present. 3rd rev. ed., Eds. W. J. Burke and Will D. Howe. New York: Crown, 1972.

American Literary Manuscripts. Austin: University of Texas Press, 1960.

American Literature Abstracts. Eds. James K. Bower and Richard Van Der Beets. Los Angeles: California State Colleges, 1967-1972.

Articles on American Literature. Comp. Lewis Gaston Leary. Durham, N.C.: Duke University Press, 1954.

Articles on American Literature, 1950-1967. Comp. Lewis Gaston Leary. Durham, N.C.: Duke University Press, 1972.

Ayer Directory of Publications. Philadelphia: Ayer Press, 1975.

Bernhardt, William, ed. Granger's Index to Poetry. 5th ed., New York: Columbia University Press, 1962.

________. ________. 6th ed., 1973.

Bibliographic Index. Monthly. Cumulated. New York: H. W. Wilson, 1937-.

Book Review Index. Quarterly Cumulations. Detroit: Gale Research, 1965-.

Book Review Digest. Annual Cumulations. New York: H. W. Wilson, 1905-.

Books in Print. Author and Title Indexes. Annual. New York: R. R. Bowker.

Brewton, John and Sara Brewton, eds. Index to Children's Poetry. New York: H. W. Wilson, 1942 and supplements.

British Books in Print: The Reference Catalog of Current Literature. 2 vols. Annual. New York: R. R. Bowker.

British Museum. Department of Printed Books. General Catalogue of Printed Books. London: London Trustees, 1931-. v. 1-.

The Cadillac Modern Encyclopedia. Ed. Max S. Shapiro. New York: Cadillac Publishing Co., 1973.

Canadian Periodical Index. Monthly with Annual and Quinquennial cumulations. Ottawa: Canadian Library Association.

Chicorel, Marietta, ed. Chicorel Index to Poetry in Anthologies and Collections in Print. New York: Chicorel, 1974.

________. Chicorel Index to the Spoken Arts on Discs, Tapes and Cassettes. New York: Chicorel, 1973.

________. Chicorel Theater Index to Plays in Anthologies, Periodicals, Discs and Tapes. New York: Chicorel, 1970.

Coan, Otis and Richard Lillard. America in Fiction. Stanford, Cal.: Stanford University Press, 1956.

________. rev. ed. Palo Alto, Cal.: Pacific Books, 1967.

Contemporary Authors. v. 4 Ed. James Ethridge. Detroit: Gale Research, 1963.

Contemporary Literary Criticism. Ed. Carolyn Riley, Detroit: Gale Research, 1975.

Contemporary Poets. Ed. Rosalie Murphy. New York: St. Martins Press, 1970.

Cook, Dorothy and Isabel S. Monro, eds. Short Story Index. New York: H. W. Wilson, 1953 and supplements.

Cumulative Book Index. New York: H. W. Wilson, 1930-.

Dart, J. Dorie, ed. International Index to Periodicals. Cumulated. New York: H. W. Wilson, 1907-.

________. Social Sciences and Humanities Index (Formerly International Index). Cumulated. New York: H. W. Wilson, 1916-74.

Davis, Lloyd and Robert Irwin. Contemporary American Poetry: A Checklist. Metuchen, N.J.: Scarecrow Press, 1975.

A Directory of American Poets, 1975 Ed. New York: Poets and Writers Inc., 1974.

Dissertation Abstracts: American Doctoral Dissertations. Cumulated Annually. Ann Arbor, Mich.: Xerox University Microfilms.

Dorsch, T. S. ed., The Year's Work in English Studies. New York: Humanities Press, 1964-1972.

Fidell, Estelle and Esther Flory, eds. Fiction Catalog. 8th ed. New York: H. W. Wilson, 1971.

________ and Dorothy Peake, eds. Play Index. New York: H. W. Wilson, 1949.

Garry, Leon, ed. The Standard Periodical Directory. New York: Oxbridge, 1973.

Havlice, Patricia. Index to Literary Biography. 2 vols. Metuchen, N.J.: Scarecrow Press, 1975.

Horden, John, ed. Annual Bibliography of English Language and Literature. Modern Humanities Research Association. London: Cambridge University Press, 1930-1974.

Index to Book Reviews in the Humanities. Annual. Williamston, Mich.: Phillip Thomson Publishing Co., 1960-.

Index to the Times. (London). London: The Times Publishing Co., 1930-.

Index Translationum. Répertoire International des Traductions. Paris: UNESCO, 1949-.

The International Who's Who in Poetry, 1958. Ed. Geoffrey Taylor-Handley. London: The Granbrook Tower Press, 1958.

J. Henry Meyer Memorial Library. Author and Title Catalog. Palo Alto, Cal.: Stanford University Libraries, 1969.

King, Betty, ed. British Humanities Index. Quarterly, Annual Cumulations. London: Library Association.

Koehmstedt, Carol, comp. Plot Summary Index. Metuchen, N.J.: Scarecrow Press, 1973.

Library Journal Book Review Index. New York: R. R. Bowker, 1967-1969.

A Library of Literary Criticism. Ed. Dorothy Nyren. New York: Frederick Ungar, 1964.

________. Ed. Dorothy Nyren Curley. New York: Frederick Ungar, 1969.

Literary and Library Prizes. New York: R. R. Bowker, 1959.

Louis, Rita V., ed. Biography Index. Cumulated. New York: H. W. Wilson, 1947-.

Magazines for Libraries. Ed. Bill Katz. New York: R. R. Bowker, 1972.

Meserole, Harrison T. et al., comps. MLA International Bibliography of Books and Articles on the Modern Languages and Literatures. New York: Modern Language Association. Annual.

New York Times Directory of the Theater. Intro., Clive Barnes. New York: New York Times Book Div., 1961.

New York Times Index. Semi-Monthly. Cumulated. New York: New York Times.

Ottemiller, John Henry, ed. Index to Plays in Collections: 1900-1962. 4th ed. New York: Scarecrow Press, 1964.

Oxford Companion to American Literature. 4th ed. Ed. James Hart. New York: Oxford University Press, 1965.

Paperbound Books in Print. Annual. New York: R. R. Bowker.

Penguin Companion to American Literature. Eds. Malcolm Bradbury, et al. New York: McGraw-Hill Book Co., 1971.

The Reader's Advisor: A Guide to the Best in Literature. Ed. Winifred F. Courtney. New York: R. R. Bowker, 1968.

The Reader's Encyclopedia of American Literature. Ed. Max J. Herzberg. New York: Thomas J. Crowell, 1962.

The Readers' Guide to Periodical Literature. Cumulated. New York: H. W. Wilson, 1905-.

Rigby, Marjory, et al. eds. Annual Bibliography of English Language and Literature. London: Cambridge University Press, 1960-.

Robbins, J. Albert, ed. American Literary Scholarship: An Annual. Durham, N.C.: Duke University Press, 1930-1974.

Sears, Minnie and Marian Shaw, eds. Essay and General Literature Index. New York: H. W. Wilson, 1934-.

Sheehy, Eugene and Kenneth Lohf, comps. Index to Little Magazines. Annual Cumulations. Denver: Alan Swallow, 1943-1967.

Twentieth Century Authors. 1st supplement. Ed. Stanley J. Kunitz. New York: H. W. Wilson, 1955.

Ulrich's International Periodicals Directory. 15th ed. New York: R. R. Bowker, 1973.

Union List of Serials. 3rd ed. New York: H. W. Wilson, 1965.

United States. Library of Congress. Archive of Recorded Poetry and Literature. Washington, D. C.: Library of Congress, 1961.

_______. National Union Catalog: A Cumulative Author List. Washington, D. C.: Library of Congress, 1953-.

_______. National Union Catalog Cumulative Author List 1968-1972 Music and Phonorecords Set. Ann Arbor, Mich.: J. W. Edwards, 1973. 5 vols.

_______. New Serial Titles, 1950-1960. (Supplement of Union List of Serials) Washington, D. C.: Library of Congress, 1973.

_______. New Serial Titles. 3rd ed. Washington, D. C.: Library of Congress, 1973.

_______. Newspapers on Microfilm. Washington, D. C.: Library of Congress, 1963.

_______. Newspapers on Microfilm: Foreign Countries, 1948-1972. Washington, D. C.: Library of Congress, 1973.

University of California. Los Angeles. Dictionary Catalog of the University Library, 1919-1962. Boston: G. K. Hall, 1963.

Whitaker's Cumulative Book List. London: J. Whitaker, 1924-.

Who's Who in American Women, 1972-1973. Chicago: A. N. Marquis Co., 1971.

Woodress, James Leslie, ed. Dissertations in American Literature. Durham, N. C.: Duke University Press, 1962.

Zulauf, Sander W. and Irwin H. Weiser, eds. Index of American Periodical Verse: 1971. Metuchen, N. J.: Scarecrow Press, 1973-. (Annual.)

AUTHOR INDEX